Paul Faust

Does Aid Contribute to Sustainable Development Goals?

Empirical Evidence from a Donor Comparison

Anchor Academic
Publishing

Faust, Paul: Does Aid Contribute to Sustainable Development Goals? Empirical Evidence from a Donor Comparison, Hamburg, Anchor Academic Publishing 2018

Buch-ISBN: 978-3-96067-216-6
PDF-eBook-ISBN: 978-3-96067-716-1
Druck/Herstellung: Anchor Academic Publishing, Hamburg, 2018

Bibliografische Information der Deutschen Nationalbibliothek:
Die Deutsche Nationalbibliothek verzeichnet diese Publikation in der Deutschen Nationalbibliografie; detaillierte bibliografische Daten sind im Internet über http://dnb.d-nb.de abrufbar.

Bibliographical Information of the German National Library:
The German National Library lists this publication in the German National Bibliography. Detailed bibliographic data can be found at: http://dnb.d-nb.de

© Anchor Academic Publishing, Imprint der Diplomica Verlag GmbH
Hermannstal 119k, 22119 Hamburg
http://www.diplomica-verlag.de, Hamburg 2018
Printed in Germany

Contents

List of Abbreviations

BA .... Bilateral aid

DAC .... Development Assistance Committee

G1 .... Group 1 (Denmark, Finland, the Netherlands, Norway, Sweden)

G2 .... Group 2 (France, Germany, Japan, the UK, the US)

GDP .... Gross domestic product

GMM .... Generalised method of moments

GNI .... Gross national income

HDI .... Human Development Indicator

IMF .... International Monetary Fund

INSCR .... Integrated Network for Societal Conflict Research

MA .... Multilateral aid

MDG .... Millennium Development Goals

MENA .... Middle East and North Africa (region)

NGO .... Non-governmental organisation

ODA .... Official Development Aid

OECD .... Organisation for Economic Co-operation and Development

OLS .... Ordinary least squares

SDG .... Sustainable Development Goal

SSA .... Sub-Saharan Africa

UK .... United Kingdom

UN .... United Nations

UNDP .... United Nations Development Programme

US .... United States of America

USD .... US Dollar

WDI .... World Development Indicators

List of Tables

List of Figures

List of Appendices

1 Introduction

No Poverty, *Zero Hunger*, *Good Health*, *Well-being* and *Quality Education* - these are the first priorities of the Sustainable Development Goals (SDGs) that were launched jointly by all UN Member States on 1 January 2016. The agenda of this agreement contains 17 main goals with a total of 169 targets and is dedicated to improving global living conditions and to address issues of environmental and economical sustainability with a planning horizon through to 2030. Development assistance from economically advanced countries, also referred to as aid, is one of the major means to provide financing for countries with less developed economies that face severe social problems and which often cannot handle these problems alone.

Half a century ago, several major industrialised countries began to launch large aid programmes after establishing the Development Assistance Committee (DAC) that serves as a platform for dialogue and discussion about the way international donors can contribute most effectively to the development of economically poorer countries. Since 1964, aid flows from DAC member countries are recorded as Official Development Assistance (ODA) and corresponding data is made publicly available. The number of donors, as well as the amount of funds, is consistently growing, reaching a maximum of almost USD 95 billion spent by 30 member countries in 2014. Over certain periods of time, aid payments accounted for a large share of the domestic economy of single recipient countries. In the most extreme cases, aid flows from various donors added up to more than 50% of the government budget – often spanning several years.

Such extensive monetary flows that aim to improve economic and social conditions in a broad range of developing countries were unknown until that time, leaving open the question of the resulting effect. Because the topic also implies a moral importance due to the donors' commitment to eliminate global poverty and inequality, the topic immediately attracted world-wide interest among the research society. The first studies dealing with the subject appeared almost simultaneously as the first aid flows were disbursed. These studies assess the possible impact of aid, theoretically based on former growth models. As soon as first data became available, researchers began to directly estimate the effect of aid on economic parameters. By now, the topic of aid effectiveness covers an immense amount of contributions with a variety of different research fields.

Estimation methods, as well as quality and availability of data on developing countries have improved over the time. However, despite the emergence of more accurate methodology and an increasing number of scientific contributions, the entire history of research on this topic is accompanied by a lack of consensus. On the one hand, several studies find that aid has a significant positive impact on growth, whereas an equally large share of contributions cannot find an effect at all, or even demonstrate a negative correlation between aid and growth. The disagreement among researchers is not only consistent over time, but also across different estimation methods and even between studies that apply the same approaches based on identical data. The perennial debate that has emerged over the past twenty years particularly leaves the reader with the impression that research in this area is going around in circles. Studies that take up the finding of a preceding investigations, apply small changes to the original approach and end up with a different result largely shape the image of the latest aid effectiveness literature – one can therefore conclude that the question whether aid as a positive impact on growth or not still remains unanswered.

It is certain, however, that aid in general is falling short of the initial expectations that donors and first researchers had. Therefore, a wide range of the literature aims to find out why aid does not show to have the desired effect. Several studies find that aid increases non-productive government expenditures instead of benefitting the poor. Others argue that aid only shows to be effective when directed to recipient countries with a high level of institutional quality and good policies, and conclude that funds have largely been transferred to the wrong countries. A further avenue of research that has developed over the past decades pursues a different objective than estimating the effect of aid: By analysing the pattern of aid flows, the aid allocation literature determines the main driving forces behind the donors' choice of recipient countries. Resulting insights prove to be plausible explanations for the missing effectiveness of aid. The parameters that presumably shape the allocation decisions are either related to the recipient, such as humanitarian needs, institutional quality or the level of economic openness; or to the donor, e.g. political and economic interests or ties with recipients that have formerly been colonised by the donor.

One of the major conclusions of one strand of the aid allocation literature, most of which published during the past 15 years, is that there are striking differences among donors regarding their prioritisation of recipient needs or their own objectives. Several studies find that major industrialised countries, such as the US, Japan or France, put less emphasis on recipient needs and more on their own objectives. In contrast, aid from multilateral donors or smaller bilateral donors, such as Scandinavian countries or the Netherlands, is considered to be far less driven by economic or power-political interests and proves to be distributed with a high regard for the different recipient-related parameters.

Taking this observation into consideration, it appears evident that the effectiveness of aid, equal to the pattern of allocation, differs among donors. Yet, nearly all investigations focus on the effect of aggregated aid – i.e. total aid funds from all donors. Only in recent years, research begins to consider this issue, mostly distinguishing between the impact of bilateral and multilateral aid. Empirical evidence on potential differences in aid effectiveness between single bilateral donors, however, remains very limited. Because bilateral aid accounts for most of the total supplied funds, further research on this topic is indispensable.

Consequently, the main research objective of this thesis is to investigate whether the insight of the aid allocation literature, i.e. bilateral donors differ significantly regarding the motives behind allocating aid, can be applied to determine measurable differences in aid effectiveness. In other words, are differences in the way distinct donor countries allocate aid large enough to result in quantitative differences in the impact on development of recipient countries? The answer to this question could offer an explanation for why aid research often fails to find a positive effect of aid. And more importantly, it could provide insight on the types of aid that appear to be unrelated with development and those that show a positive impact on recipient countries.

In order to estimate differences between bilateral donors, this study forms two groups that are assumed to allocate aid in a significantly different manner – an approach that is not applied up to the present. The first group comprises Denmark, Finland, the Netherlands, Norway and Sweden; all of which seem to exclude personal interest and to put great emphasis on recipient needs. France, Germany, Japan, the United States of America (US) and the United Kingdom (UK) form the second group as bilateral donors that are considered to allocate aid with high regard to their own objectives. To determine the possible difference in aid effectiveness between these two donor groups, the aim of this thesis is to follow the latest and established strategies of estimating the effect of aid on growth in a first place.

As several recent studies argue that growth is not the only appropriate measure of development, this thesis additionally investigates the impact of aid on the two most often researched social indicators. These are infant mortality, as a key indicator for heath standards, and primary education to measure the quality of the educational system. Both of these indicators are explicitly included in the agenda of the eight Millennium Development Goals (MDGs) of 2000 and are concrete targets of the current SDGs. Thus, an analysis of the effect on the two indicators also covers a more concrete answer to the question whether aid contributes to sustainable development goals.

Moreover, because the literature does not agree on whether or not multilateral aid is more effective than bilateral aid, the analyses of this study are accompanied by a further differentiation between these two types of aid. In addition to the separate analysis of two bilateral donor groups, this kind of disaggregating aid offers a further opportunity to decompose aid into potentially ineffective or beneficial types. As bilateral aid comprises both donor groups of the main investigation, this additional analysis enables a direct comparison of aggregated and disaggregated aid flows, which possibly achieves more valuable results.

The investigations of this study consider two further insights of the previous literature. The first one is that aid is assumed to affect development with a partially large time lag. The rationale behind this assumption is that development assistance largely comprises projects in areas such as infrastructure, energy, education or health, which require a long implementation period until they may achieve benefits. Second, several studies suggest that the aid allocation of major donors has significantly changed since the end of the Cold War, implying changes in the underlying motives. As the latter finding indicates that aid effectiveness increases after 1989, additional estimations shall reduce the observation period to 1990-2014.

In order to gradually answer these research questions, the study first presents a detailed investigation of the existing literature, beginning with a section that outlines the origin and history of the research field. This section aims at identifying problems and solutions associated with the estimation of aid effects and additionally addresses the current debate on the impact of aid on growth. The closer inspection of the recent research covers studies from the last 20 years; the aid effectiveness literature has seen a remarkable upswing during this period, which has led to a persistent discussion. In a next step, the literature review shifts the focus away from the aid-growth debate to the usage of alternative development indicators for measuring the impact of aid.

A further section then discusses those investigations that determine the pattern of aid allocation. Studies of this strand of literature provide an important theoretical foundation for this thesis, i.e. the indication that aid effectiveness might differ between donors. Investigations of this kind also demonstrate changes in motives for providing aid after the end of the Cold War. The insights of the aid allocation literature lead to a final section that discusses the approaches and results of previous studies that attempt to measure differences in aid effectiveness among donors. Following the literature review, a separate chapter utilises the obtained insights in order to draw implications for the subsequent analysis and to precisely define the research objectives of this study.

A descriptive analysis initiates the empirical part of this study. After describing the applied data and corresponding issues, the main section of this chapter attempts to confirm the findings of the aid allocation literature in the case of the donors that are analysed in this study. An investigation of the temporal development of each donor's aid flows, followed by a more detailed analysis of the individual pattern of aid allocation shall amplify the evidence achieved from the literature. Subsequent cross-sectional estimations of the actual aid effects provide reader with a first approximation of the results among different donors. The analysis of cross-country data based on ordinary least squares (OLS) method is among the first approaches for estimating the effect of aid, and is still applied by a number of recent studies. The initial assessment is divided into three parts. The first section identifies donor-specific aid effects on growth

4

as the indicator that is most-often applied for estimating the impact on development in recipient countries. The second part observes both infant mortality and primary completion as social indicators. A final section approximates how aid effects vary in the post-1989 period after the end of the Cold War.

The application of cross-sectional data, however, is for several reasons afflicted with a certain inaccuracy, compared to more sophisticated estimation strategies based on panel data that have emerged over the past decades. The main estimation method of choice, therefore, is a generalised method of moments (GMM) based dynamic panel analysis. Chapter 6, as the main of the empirical analysis, begins by discussing the benefits of the GMM dynamic panel data approach in contrast to cross-sectional investigation. Subsequently, the effect on growth and on both social indicators is reassessed. As the application of GMM estimators is not free from bias either, a third section of chapter 6 tests for robustness of the panel data approach. This is based on simple OLS methodology and a fixed effects (FE) estimator, both of which are also applied in recent research. A further step is to derive policy implications from the obtained results, and chapter 8 concludes.

2 The Debate on Aid Effectiveness

Following the establishment of the Development Assistance Committee in 1960, nearly all the major developed countries started extensive aid programmes with the objective of alleviating global poverty (cf. Doucouliagos and Paldam 2006: 227). Shortly afterwards, first researchers began to assess the effects of aid against the high expectations of the donors. The first studies were published at the end of the 1960s and the early 1970s. Since then, a great variety of researchers have been dealing with the question whether and to which extent development assistance impacts economic growth of recipient countries. Underlying theories and the methodical procedure to filter out the effect of aid have been reconsidered and adapted to more sophisticated empirical approaches several times up to the present.

More surprisingly, but very characteristic for the aid research, the numerous outcomes for the effect of aid vary to a high extent and are inconsistent in sign and degree up until now. For this reason, and for the great number of contributions in this area, multiple studies attempt to categorise the research field by classifying contributions by their findings or the methodical framework put to use. Scientific approaches from the first decades of research have repeatedly been refined and further developed and hence are less relevant for the empirical part of this thesis. Yet, their contributions are useful for understanding the nature of the aid effectiveness debate and shall, thus, be summarised briefly. Because the most influential and still discussed studies have been published over the past 20 years, their procedure and findings shall be analysed in more detail.[1]

At the beginning of the debate in this field, aid effectiveness was generally seen in an economical context. After initial attempts to analyse the impact on more precise macroeconomic determinants such as savings and investment, the approach of analysing the direct impact on economic growth has prevailed so far in this strand of the literature. A first section explains this development and the predominant strand of research, the aid-growth literature. Recently, several contributions consider the impact of aid on social indicators in addition to growth. A second section illustrates the reasons behind this choice, as well as the approaches and outcomes of influential studies in this field.

2.1 The aid-growth literature

The first contributions from the early 1960s mostly focus on the estimated capital required by developing countries. Theoretically based on the Harrod-Domar growth model, these studies address the relationship between foreign assistance and total savings with the underlying assumption that filling up the saving gap implies higher

---

[1]Extensive investigations of the first decades of research can, for instance, be found in Hansen und Tarp (2000) or the meta-analyses of Doucouliagos and Paldam (2006, 2009).

investments and therefore an increase in growth. With a positive expectation towards the effect of aid on growth, they assume that aid payments contribute in an equal amount to the developing countries' savings and thus investment, such as Rosenstein-Rodan (1961: 136), to name one of the most influential studies of this period.

The arguments of a subsequent strand of the literature likewise draw on the effect on savings. However, questioning the high expectations of the previous literature, these studies find out a negative impact of foreign assistance on domestic savings of developing countries. Since they attempt to determine the extent of aid for the first time by applying cross-sectional or time series analyses, they are often regarded the first contributions to the aid effectiveness literature (cf. Clemens et al. 2012: 591). The earliest publication of this strand of the aid-savings literature, Griffin and Enos (1970: 320), states that the former expected relationship between aid and savings would be too simple and that a general negative tendency between foreign assistance and domestic savings points towards a negative effect on growth. Weisskopf (1972: 37) even concludes that the effect of aid on ex ante domestic savings would be significantly negative.

Soon afterwards, Papanek (1972, 1973) marks an early turning point in the literature by shifting away the focus from analysing the effect on savings towards directly measuring the impact of aid on growth. He argues that savings had so far been determined by subtracting inflows from investment, which would lead to a self-explanatory negative correlation (cf. Papanek 1972: 945-947). Considering the issue of causality between low savings in least developed countries (LDC) and high aid payments for the first time, he questions the validity of previous results. Furthermore, he disputes the approaches of his predecessors because of their aggregation of all foreign inflows. He attempts to separate these, resulting in a regression for predicting the various effects of aid, savings, investment and other components of foreign inflows on growth (Papanek 1973: 121) and concludes that there is a strongly significant correlation between aid and growth (ibid.: 129).

The approach of Papanek is taken up by a series of subsequent studies that investigate the effect of aid on either investment. Amongst these is Mosley (1980: 81-84), who introduces a further methical advancement to the aid literature by instrumenting for aid in a two stage least squares regression. He comes to the conclusion that the overall relation between aid and growth is negative and insignificant, but positive when only considering the poorest countries (ibid.: 89-90). Although several subsequent publications take up this procedure, the actual impact of aid remains controversial: Levy (1988: 1781-1787), for instance, finds a strongly significant positive impact on both investment and growth in African countries. Snyder (1993: 484) even reports an overall positive effect of aid after controlling for population growth of the recipient countries.

On the opposite side, various studies find that aid and growth prove are unrelated, such as Mosley et al. (1987: 636).

The recent literature, considering the current status, is introduced by the work of Boone (1996). With the help of more complete data, he performs panel data analyses with five-year averages while controlling for country specific effects (ibid.: 305). Moreover, he uses three new instruments for dealing with potential endogeneity in the regressors and analyses aid effects on growth, infant mortality, life expectancy and primary school attendance (ibid. 308-309). Boone (1996: 322-323) arrives at the conclusion that aid does not show to have any significant effect on neither of the parameters. Instead, he observes a connection between aid and higher total consumption. He states at the same time, however, that there is no evidence that higher consumption would benefit the poor (ibid.: 315). Boone's findings have been addressed by many studies up to the present. The literature that has emerged since then can be classified into three strands of studies – in the following also termed studies of strand 1-3.[2] A first line of studies finds a positive impact of aid under certain circumstances, such as the existence of specific policies or relations between the donor country and the recipient. A second series of studies, strand 2, confirms the results of Boone, i.e. aid and growth are uncorrelated. On the contrary, a third strand of the literature determines a positive effect of aid that holds regardless of certain conditions.

The first strand, which Clemens et al. (2012) term the "conditional strand" (p. 592), comprises several of the most influential studies of the aid-growth literature. These studies reflect Boone's results of an absent effect of aid on growth in a total sample, but determine a positive effect of aid only under certain circumstances and, thus, imply opportunities of (re)structuring aid flows in an effective manner. The arguably best-known example is Burnside and Dollar (2000), which extend the instrumentation strategy by including an interaction term of aid and economic policies. After determining a significantly positive coefficient of this variable, Burnside and Dollar (2000: 857) conclude that aid works better in countries that feature strong economic policies and institutions. Many subsequent papers, for example Easterly (2003: 24) or Clemens et al. (2004: 8), highlight the great influence of Burnside and Dollar (2000) on both research and the policies of major aid organisations, such as the World Bank and other multilateral development banks. Furthermore, there are various papers that confirm the relationship between good policies and the effectiveness of aid on growth, as for example Alvi et al. (2008: 702). Other studies belonging to this strand of the literature identify a positive effect of aid on growth in countries that are, for instance, geographically located outside the tropics (cf. Dalgaard et al. 2004: 201) or in a longer period of peace (cf. Collier and Doller 2002: 1135).

---

[2]The following categorisation of the recent aid into three strands is inspired by Clemens et al. (2012: 592-593) and extended up to the present.

A further number of publications can be assigned to a second strand due to their common conclusion that aid and growth are unrelated, regardless of certain circumstances. To this category belongs Roodman (2007: 266), who tests the robustness of several influential first strand studies - amongst them Burnside and Dollar (2000) and Dalgaard et al. (2004). He concludes that all outcomes of the analysed studies are characterised by fragility and that aid "is probably not a fundamentally decisive factor for development" (ibid.: 275). One of the most prominent publications of the past decade, as many studies highlight (cf. Clemens et al. 2012: 595), can also be found in this category: Rajan and Subramanian (2008) analyse the causal relation between aid and growth based on both cross-sectional and panel data analyses in a comprehensive way. They test for several assumptions, such as the decisive role of good policies and the geographical location, as well as the timing of the impact of aid; and conclude that aid over all their findings has no significant positive effect on growth (ibid.: 660).

Opposed to the findings of the second cluster, the third strand of the recent literature reveals an overall positive impact of aid on growth. An early influential work is Hansen and Tarp (2001), who also address the insight of Burnside and Dollar (2000) that aid would only work in good policy environments. They are the first within the aid literature to apply a GMM estimator. This procedure has attracted particular attention within the aid literature and is adopted by many subsequent studies, such as the aforementioned Rajan and Subramanian (2008: 658-660).[3] Hansen and Tarp (2001: 552) retain the strategy of instrumenting for policy, but modify the original set of instruments and include lagged values of the aid regressors for modelling the assumption of non-linear returns of aid. Accounting for both original least squares and GMM-estimations, Hansen and Tarp (2001: 563) conclude that aid has a positive and significant effect on growth via investment.

Gomanee et al. (2005A: 1068) arrive at the same result in a sample of 25 countries in Sub-Saharan Africa (SSA). Several publications of the past years can also be classified as studies of the third strand. Arndt et al. (2010: 19-21), as well as Clemens et al. (2012: 608) draw on the original specification of Rajan and Subramanian (2008) demonstrate a modest but general positive effect of aid on growth. Both studies have in common that they turn away from GMM-estimations, although this method has been recognised as a sound practice in the aid literature since the work of Hansen and Tarp (2001). The robustness check, carried out in section 6.3, revisits this recent doubt about the applicability of GMM-estimators. Finally, Brückner (2013: 131-135) also achieves a significantly positive effect of aid. Remarkable for his approach is that he tackles the endogeneity problem by explicitly estimating the effect of an increase in gross domestic product (GDP) per capita growth in recipient countries on the amount of foreign aid in a first step.

---

[3]Chapter 6 contains detailed information on the GMM approach and its benefits, as well as its limitations.

2.2 Looking beyond the effect of growth

The investigation of the impact of aid on economic growth in developing countries may be considered the classical strand of the aid effectiveness literature. As indicated in the introduction, however, there are several reasons why the growth effect should not be the only criteria to use for measuring the effectiveness of aid. Several researches of the past two decades shift their focus towards investigating the effect of aid on different indicators of human development. These studies include key indicators in the areas of health and education, as well as poverty indices. In the following, this section analyses research in this rather novel field with a focus on the underlying theoretical assumptions for turning towards a focus on social indicators.

A fundamental objective of investigating the effectiveness of aid regarding its impact on social indicators is to evaluate whether it contributes to achieving the goals that have jointly been defined by the United Nations (UN) member countries. At the UN Millennium Summit in 2000, both developing and developed countries met for the first time to establish a common target catalogue for promoting international development, labelled Millennium Development Goals. These targets include improvements in the fields of global health, education, poverty reduction, equality, as well as peace and freedom promotion with an objective horizon of 15 years (cf. UNDP 2003: 31). After the expiration of the 15 years planning horizon, the common goals were redefined in 2016 and laid down in the 17 Sustainable Development Goals of the UN (cf. DESA: 2016).[4] Because aid is expected to be an essential instrument for achieving these goals, several studies devote to explicitly analysing the correlation between aid and the achievement of MDGs, e.g. Dreher et al. (2008: 292) or Masud and Yontcheva (2005: 3).

Apart from the rather self-evident objective of assessing the ability of aid to contribute to commonly defined goals, there are more reasons why indicators for social welfare are suitable for measuring aid effectiveness. First, several studies point out that aid targeted towards improvements in social areas may only have an impact on growth in the very long run. Arndt et al. (2015: 9) demonstrate this time-lagged growth effect of aid based on the example of the education field. They consider only those kinds of aid which are directed at improving educational quality and show that higher school attendance rates, caused by these aid flows, may only have an observable influence on growth after a considerable share of beneficiaries has passed through the education system. Boone (1996: 293) already stresses that infant mortality, as a key indicator for health, would respond quickly to improved conditions. In line with this, Dreher et al. (2008) argue that social indicators would be "more specific outcome variables than growth" (292).

A further line of arguments emphasises the high explanatory power of social indicators

---

[4]Annex A shows provides an overview of the agendas of both MDGs and SDGs.

in measuring welfare gains of the poor. Gomanee et al. (2005B: 300) point out that increases in aggregate economic growth do not necessarily reflect better conditions of the poor; which is, however, a main target of aid. For this reason, they attempt to capture a broader measure of total welfare benefits by focusing on improvements in both infant mortality and the Human Development Indicator (HDI). Chong et al. (2009: 60), as well as Alvi and Senbeta (2012: 955) share the same position. In contrast to their predecessors, however, they both rely on poverty headcount and poverty gap indices. They argue that this procedure gives indication on income distribution and equality, representing additional important factors of development besides a countries' average economic growth (ibid.: 957).

Corresponding to the overall conclusion of the classical aid-growth literature, the findings of this strand of the aid effectiveness research are also diverse. However, a majority of the studies report positive effects of aid. Recent findings, furthermore, show a clear trend towards more optimistic findings. Boone (1996: 312-313) is the first to incorporate social indicators into his estimations with the purpose of measuring improvements in the living conditions of the poor. For this purpose, he chooses infant mortality, life expectancy, as well as primary schooling. He finds out that aid does not significantly influence neither of the variables. As mentioned in the previous section, Boone rather observes a higher consumption rate correlating with aid payments and concludes that these results "are consistent with a model where politicians maximize welfare of a wealthy elite" (ibid.: 322).

In line with this finding, Chong et al. (2009: 79) are not able to detect a significant impact of aid on their measures for poverty. This negative overall picture of the relation between aid and social indicators, however, is only supported in a small number of studies. Gomanee et al. (2005B: 305), as well as Masud and Yontcheva (2005: 13) find that aid reduces infant mortality. While Gomanee et al. (2005B, 302) use total aggregated aid flows, Masud and Yontcheva (2005: 9) distinguish between bilateral aid (BA) and aid from non-governmental organisations (NGOs) and demonstrate that only the latter has a significant effect.

Particularly in recent years, a predominantly positive perception of aid towards improving social welfare has become apparent. Dreher et al. (2008: 299), for instance, show that aid specifically assigned to the education sector contributes significantly to higher school enrolment rates. In a similar approach, Mishra and Newhouse (2009: 865) consider aid in the health sector and find that this type of aid contributes to alleviating infant mortality. The two latter mentioned investigations apply a separation of aid flows by their purpose. Because their target is to investigate only the assistance for education and health respectively, they separate these aid types from the total aid numbers. Section 3.2 discusses the approach of disaggregating aid according to assignment in more detail.

Even without separating aid, Alvi and Senbeta (2012: 965) determine a negative and significant impact of total aid flows on both poverty gap and poverty rate. Finally, Arndt et al. (2015: 10-13) apply a two-step analysis with intermediate outcomes of aid, amongst them measures for health and education, that contribute accumulatively to final outcomes, represented by GDP growth and poverty indices. They conclude that aid has an average positive long-run effect on the final outcomes by stimulating the intermediate outcomes, such as better health and education conditions (ibid.: 15).

2.3 Evidence from donor investigations

So far, one major conclusion can be drawn from the literature analysis: A larger share of the research on aid effectiveness fails to find a significantly positive impact of aggregated aid flows (cf. Rajan and Subramanian 2008 and 2011, Burnside and Dollar 2000 or Easterly et al. 2004). For this reason, a major current research goal in this field is to gain insight into the reasons for the apparent failure of total aggregated aid. Section 2.1 already describes one empirical procedure for this purpose; by instrumenting for certain characteristics of the developing countries, such as their institutional quality or climatic circumstances, scholars try to find out under which circumstances aid generates positive effects and when it appears to not have any significant impact. Studies of this type have already had a strong influence on policy, such as the shift of aid allocation of major agencies towards countries with a better policy environment (cf. Easterly et al. 2004: 774).

A further possibility of understanding why overall aid apparently does not achieve its goals is to look at the single development assistance flows separately, i.e. disaggregating aid numbers. The underlying assumption behind this approach is that different aid, or aid flows to different countries, can vary in their effectiveness. The disaggregation, again, can be done in different ways. The two major differences of these approaches are the following: One way is to consider the underlying objective behind the different aid flows and, consequently, to distinguish between the different purposes of aid, which are defined by the donor. Many studies apply such a procedure, amongst them Headey (2008: 169) and Clemens et al. (2012: 594), who subtract the share of humanitarian aid from total ODA with the purpose of only considering the types of aid that are targeted at increasing economic growth, or Dreher et al. (2008: 300), who find a positive impact of aid and education indicators while considering only those aid flows that were assigned to the education sector. This thesis, however, does not apply such a procedure. Section 4.2 provides the argumentation behind this choice.

Beside this kind of disaggregation, there is a second established way of breaking down aggregated aid: Various studies subdivide aid flows according to the way they are allocated to recipient countries. This type of studies is often referred to as the aid allocation literature (cf. Harrigan and Wang 2011: 1282). One objective of several of these investigations is to determine a pattern of aid allocation that is most effective regarding the aggregated increase of welfare in developing countries. Another major target of this kind of research is to determine factors that prove to be decisive for the choice of the individual donor's allocation. Such factors, on the one hand, can be derived at the recipient country level - humanitarian needs or the degree of poverty are examples for this. But they can also be investigated from the donor country perspective and include factors such as political or commercial interests. Finally, these approaches are expanded by several studies in order to compare the aid allocation of different donors. These studies argue that the patterns of aid allocation vary significantly between different donors. Some of them conclude that inadequate aid allocations, presumably caused by personal donor motives, are a major cause for the ineffectiveness of total aggregated aid. The following section depicts this strand of the literature and their implications for this thesis in more detail, with a focus on those studies that devote to determining differences between different donors.

The conclusions of the aid allocation literature, however, do not provide information on the eventual effects of different patterns of aid flows. Or put differently: They provide insights about differences in aid allocations of different donors (qualitatively), but do not quantify these. Only a few studies so far attempt a quantification of aid impacts separated by donors. Their measurements are mostly based on implications of the aid allocation literature. A further section depicts these approaches and their results.

2.3.1 The aid allocation literature: Deriving donor interests

To begin with, this section outlines the main approaches and findings of the aid allocation literature. Implications derived from this strand of research serve as the main theoretical foundation of this thesis. Similar to the aid-growth literature depicted in section 2.1, there are numerous studies contributing to this research field with a history that goes back to the 1970s.[5]

McKinlay and Little (1977) already elaborate on explaining the allocation of official bilateral aid by the example of the US development assistance. They develop five models for each possible type of donor interest and analyse, based on a cross-sectional analysis of the period 1960-1970, which of the models correlates most with the allocation of US aid over this period (ibid.: 68-72). The interests represented by the five models include fostering development, political stability and democracy in developing countries, but also (own) economical, security and power-political interests of the US. The authors find

---

[5]For further reading: Harrigan and Wang (2011: 1282-1283) provide a detailed review on the aid allocation literature, including early research.

(ibid.: 78) that the model of the last-mentioned set of interests is the most appropriate one for describing the choice of allocation. They arrive at the drastic conclusion that the high explanatory potential of US power-political and security interests behind its aid allocation shows that aid is mainly used to maintain the balance of power between donor and recipient and that it "permits aid to be seen as a dimension of imperialism" (McKinlay and Little 1977: 80).

Many previous studies come to similar conclusions. In their influential work, Collier and Dollar (2001: 1791-1793) calculate a poverty efficient allocation of aid and conclude that the current allocation, driven by other motives than total poverty alleviation, is far from this optimum. They also demonstrate that the actual aid allocation would be more efficient with a stronger focus on the quality of policies and institutions of the recipient countries (ibid.). According to their conclusions, a stronger allocation emphasis towards countries with a high poverty rate and sound policies would be necessary for achieving the MDGs (ibid.: 1800). This is in line with the findings of those studies that instrument for policy, as depicted in section 2.1. Equally responding to this result, Harrigan and Wang (2011: 1291) calculate that only 14,8% of the total US aid is allocated on the basis of good policies. Kilby and Dreher (2010: 340) likewise state that donor motives are able to impact the effectiveness of aid significantly. In this context, Alesina and Dollar (2000: 45-46) show that bilateral donors provide more aid to countries that have been former colonies, suggesting that geopolitical and economic interest play a determinant role for their aid allocation. Berthélemy (2006A: 188) adds that, beside the geopolitical and post-colonial variables, the export intensity of bilateral donors is also correlated positively with the bilateral aid allocation.

Let us now turn to those studies of the aid allocation literature that attempt to outline differences between the allocation of certain donor countries. As an early example, Dollar and Levin (2006: 2036) analyse differences in aid allocation between multilateral agencies and bilateral donors. Among their findings is that bilateral aid appears to have a weaker relationship with both democracy and rule of law compared to aid from multilateral donors. Furthermore, they point out that MA is more effectively targeted to poorer countries (ibid.). As already pointed out by their predecessors, they emphasize the important role of former colonial ties between rich industrialised countries and the recipient countries, as well as the high correlation between aid and exports of bilateral donors (cf. Dollar and Levin 2006: 2044). These results are echoed by Harrigan and Wang (2011: 1288), who investigate the aid allocation of the US compared to other multilateral and bilateral donors. They find that bilateral donors put less emphasis on good policy environments and recipient needs than multilateral agencies and illustrate this by the example of the two countries with the highest aid donations, the US and Japan, which allocate only a low proportion of their aid according to recipient needs and good policy (ibid.).

Looking more closely at the causes for the distribution of US aid flows in the region of Middle East and North Africa (MENA), they find a high positive correlation between their measurement for donor interest and aid directed towards Israel and Jordan – the main allies of the US in this region. Opposed to this, their coefficients for Iran, Sudan and Syria, as countries that are typically considered hostile to US policy over the observation period of this study, show a significantly negative and sign. By this example, they demonstrate the high relevance of strategic interests in the pattern of bilateral aid allocation. However, Berthélemy (2006B) adds to this discussion that "multilateral aid allocations are not themselves immune to the influence of donor self-interest variables [...]" (107). His estimations show that that the commercial interest of several important bilateral donors influences the allocation pattern of major multilateral agencies significantly (ibid.: 99-101).

Several subsequent studies depict the orientation of major bilateral aid donors towards own goals instead towards recipients' needs or their achievements in good governance. Dreher et al. (2011: 1955-1956), e.g., compare the aid allocation of countries that have launched their first aid programmes during recent years, such as Brazil or Korea, with those of the traditional DAC countries. Against the background that the newly emerged donors are often criticised as being self-centred, they illustrate that DAC donors show a very similar pattern to these, characterised by a correlation between aid flows and donor exports, as well as their disregarding of the level of corruption in recipient counties. Alesina and Dollar (2000: 46-47) demonstrate the geopolitical interest behind aid flows of main industrialised countries. By analysing the UN voting pattern of recipient countries, they find a strong correlation between these votes and the aid allocation of all the major industrialised donor countries, i.e. France, Germany, Japan, the UK and the US. According to their argumentation, this result reflects that aid is a measure to pursue strategic goals (ibid.).

At a different point, Alesina and Dollar (2000: 42) argue that the four Scandinavian countries Denmark, Finland, Norway and Sweden show a great similarity in their allocation of aid. The authors find that these countries, opposed to the industrialised countries, put a high emphasis on the needs of poor countries and the rewarding of good policies (ibid.: 50). At the same conclusion arrives Berthélemy (2006A, 190-191). After analysing the trade intensity of bilateral donors with the individual recipient countries, he groups donors according to their orientation towards either own interests, or those of the developing country. In addition to the Scandinavian countries, he classifies Switzerland and the Netherlands as altruistic donors, i.e. they decide about the allocation of assistance regardless their bilateral relation with the recipient. The distribution of the beforementioned industrialised, he depicts further, differs strongly from this. Especially for France, Italy, Japan and the US, he finds a more egoistic pattern compared to other donors (cf. Berthélemy 2006A: 193). Dreher et al. (2010:

60), who conduct an analysis of both Swedish bilateral and NGO aid, find that Swedish BA is not correlated with increases in exports. Furthermore, they show that the recipient countries' resource endowments correlate negatively with both the Swedish NGO aid and BA (ibid.). One would therefore assume a strong orientation of the Swedish aid towards recipient needs.

In the context of different donor motives and their connection to aid effectiveness, one further finding of the aid allocation shall be highlighted at this point: In their analysis of aid allocated during the 1980s, Schraeder et al. (1998: 321-322) already expect that donor motives would change significantly after the end of the Cold War. As a reason for this, they assume that the great role of political ideology in the allocation of aid would decrease with tensions relieving between the Eastern and the Western bloc. Dollar and Levin (2006: 2044) take this argument into consideration and find that the correlation between aid flows and economic governance of recipient countries turns for both bilateral and multilateral aid (MA) from negative in the 1980s to positive in an observation period of 2000-2003. Harrigan and Wang (2011: 1290) confirm this outcome only partially: They determine that all donor countries, apart from Canada and the US, have placed a stronger focus on recipient needs after 1989 than during the Cold War. However, they also show that only a smaller share of the donors has changed the emphasis on good policies after the end of 1989. Among the countries who do not appear to have changed in this regard are Japan, the US as well as multilateral donors.

To sum up this section: A closer examination of the aid allocation literature reveals that there are considerable differences in the way different donors distribute aid amongst recipient countries. Individual donor motives, colonial ties and historical circumstances are conceivable reasons for this. Moreover, several studies distinguish between those donors that feature a recipient oriented "fair" allocation of aid and others that tend to distribute their aid with a strong orientation towards own goals. Studies of this type are conducted against the background of the aid effectiveness debate and attempt to provide an explanation of the apparent failure of aggregated aid.

2.3.2 Determining donor differences

Insights of the aid allocation literature indicate that effects resulting from development assistance can strongly differ among donors. One possibility to quantitatively test this argument is to investigate the impact of aid on final outcomes while looking at the aid flows from distinct donors separately. Some studies so far aim at identifying such donor-related aid effectiveness. The most commonly analysed type of donor differences, in this context, is the one between multilateral and bilateral donors. Headey (2008: 170), for instance, finds that the effect of MA on growth is nearly twice as high as the effect of BA. Beside the separation between the two kinds of donors, he also uses a different measure for aid, as mentioned before: He focuses on aid that is intended to increase production by subtracting flows of humanitarian aid and, additionally, excluding the repayments flows of aid loans (ibid.: 164). This empirical strategy differs from the most commonly used approach of considering total net flows of aid.

Rajan and Subramanian (2008: 656), on the contrary, do not apply this kind of disaggregation and do not find any differences between BA and MA regarding the impact on GDP per capita growth. They even observe that neither of the two aid types has a significant positive effect over a variety of different observation periods, both in cross-sectional and dynamic panel data analyses. In addition to the observation of growth effects, there are also first contributions analysing differences between BA and MA with respect to social indicators. Following an analysis of the impact of aggregated aid on poverty measures, Alvi and Senbeta (2012: 968) distinguish between aid of bilateral and multilateral donors in a second step. Whereas total aid appears to be negatively but only moderately correlated with poverty, they cannot find any significant effect of bilateral aid on poverty alleviation. On the contrary, their estimation for the separated multilateral aid proves to be higher than the initial coefficient of aggregated aid. This suggests that the negative sign of their first estimation is exclusively determined by the capability of MA in alleviating poverty (cf. ibid.: 967-968).

In this line, Masud and Yontcheva (2005: 11-14) investigate the correlation between aid and two social indicators - children mortality for measuring health conditions, as well as adult illiteracy as an indicator for educational quality. In contrast to the above-mentioned studies, they distinguish between aid from bilateral donors on the one hand, and assistance provided by NGOs as a comparative measure. With respect to infant mortality, they find that NGO aid significantly reduces the mortality rate, while BA proves to have no influence. Regarding the illiteracy rate, they find no significant effect by neither of the two aid variables. In a next step (ibid. 17-18) they demonstrate that both NGO and bilateral aid are not negatively correlated with the recipient countries' government spending. Their conclusion is that NGO aid creates additional value to the government's efforts in the health sector, whereas the missing effectiveness of BA becomes more apparent.

Up to this point, the studies presented in this section attempt to determine differences in aid effectiveness between bilateral donor countries and non-bilateral donors, such as multilateral agencies or NGOs. The aid allocation literature, however, also suggests that there are significant differences in allocation between single donor countries. Yet, the existing literature on measuring aid effectiveness does not address this finding to a larger extent. There are nevertheless first attempts that shall be examined closely in the following. A series of estimations in Rajan and Subramanian (2008:655-656) draw on the conclusion of the aid allocation literature that some bilateral donor countries provide more effective aid than others. They only take the aid flows from the five countries Denmark, Finland, Iceland, Norway and Sweden into account. Among all their regressions for this group of donors, which include for both the growth and aid horizon variations from 10 to 40 years, Rajan and Subramanian find only one to be significantly positive (cf. ibid.).

Minoiu and Reddy (2010)[6] reach a different conclusion after investigating the differences between three different groups of bilateral donor countries. They devote to determining distinctions in aid effectiveness by systematically distinguishing between aid that is expected to promote growth on the one hand, and such types of aid that are typically regarded to have a smaller or non-existing effect on development on the other hand (28). For this purpose, they draw on the conclusions from the aid allocation literature and analyse the aid flows from donors that are supposed to allocate aid in a different manner. For the purpose of quantifying differences between donor countries, they compare one group of donor countries that are supposed to allocate aid in an altruistic manner with two control groups. The group of donors that are regarded fair comprises the four Scandinavian countries Denmark, Finland, Norway and Sweden plus the Netherlands. The two comparison groups are, first, all countries of the first group plus five further countries that are predominantly regarded to allocate their aid based on recipient needs and, second, all countries of the first group plus five countries that are assumed to allocate their aid with a focus on geostrategic aspects (30). They find that both groups of countries that are considered fair donors show a high and significant effect on the growth of recipient countries, whereas the effect of the third group that also comprises strategically oriented donors is considerably smaller (33). This result is based on both cross-sectional and dynamic panel analyses (36).

Finally, there are several investigations that quantitatively asses the above-mentioned finding of changing donor motives after the end of the Cold War. Headey (2008: 172), as well as Bearce and Tirone (2010: 843) both find that aid effectiveness increases after the end of the Cold War. They achieve this result based on different empirical approaches. While Headey (2008: 171) applies a dummy variable for the post-Cold War era to his GMM-estimations, Bearce and Tirone (2010: 842) split their sample into two separate OLS panel data estimations to analyse the pre- and post-Cold War periods respectively.

Summing up the insights from this section, the following patterns of estimated donor differences become apparent: Based on evidence from the aid allocation literature, several studies distinguish between aid flows from bilateral and multilateral donors. Regarding the difference in the effect on economic growth, there appears to be no common ground in the literature. Multilateral aid, however, turns out to be more

---

[6]The following page numbers in this paragraph, in parentheses, refer to the study of Minoiu and Reddy (2010).

effective when determining the effect on social indicators. The same finding becomes apparent when comparing aid flows from bilateral donors with those from NGOs. There is also first evidence for differences between single bilateral donor countries, which confirms the conclusions from the previous literature that different donors allocate aid in a significantly different manner based on different donor objectives.

3 Research objectives

Against the background of the remaining controversy over the impact of development assistance, this thesis aims at contributing to the aid effectiveness puzzle in the following way: The aid allocation literature suggests outcomes of aid programmes largely depend on how donors distribute aid and, consequently, on the underlying reasons and motives behind the pattern of aid allocation. Several studies also point out that there are significant differences in the way different donors allocate aid. Considering these findings, one can assume that a possibly explanation for the fact that many studies fail to find a positive effect of aggregated aid on final outcomes is that the impact of aid from single donors differs significantly. In other words, the positive effect of donors with an aid allocation based on recipient needs and development objectives could be countervailed by the effects of donors that are allocating their aid in more strategic or less development oriented manner.

The objective of this thesis is to test this hypothesis quantitatively by analysing the effects of aid from different donors separately. In doing so, this study investigates the aggregated aid flows of each donor with the objective to determine the respective total effects. This procedure offers the possibility to provide insights about which types of aid are effective in promoting development of recipient countries and which types are not.

Several studies apply a similar approach by analysing the differences in effectiveness between multilateral and bilateral aid. Their conclusions, as depicted in the previous section, lack a common consensus. Therefore, this thesis aims at contributing to this debate with a comprehensive approach. More importantly, it addresses the differences in aid effectiveness between single bilateral donors. The aid allocation literature provides strong evidence to suggest that the extent to which aid effects final outcomes differs significantly from one donor country to another. Moreover, bilateral aid accounts for almost two thirds of the total aid payments, as the subsequent section depicts. For this reason, and because aid from bilateral donors is often considered less effective than such from multilateral agencies, a closer look at the different donor countries could provide important insights. The lessons that could be learned from this approach are not only gaining insights into the puzzle of the failure of aggregated aid. In the case that certain donors prove to provide more effective aid than others, one could also draw conclusions for the effectiveness of different aid allocations and, thus, derive implications for the various aid agencies and bilateral development banks.

To allow for an accurate assessment of aid effectiveness, and to possibly determine aid that effects only a certain indicator, this study shall not only analyse the effect on growth, but also on social indicators for health and education.[7] This decision rests upon the above-mentioned fact that positive effects of aid on single social indicators might not be visible when looking at the aggregated outcome on growth, and on the fact that both the MDGs and SDGs comprise several targets regarding education as well as health (see appendix A). Moreover, there is first evidence that aid allocation during the Cold War had significantly been influenced by political interests, and that donor motives changed towards recipient needs after the end of it. Considering this observation with an analysis of the changes in aid effectiveness after the year 1989, this study also attempts to provide evidence for the importance of donor motives.

Finally, an often-discussed topic of aid effectiveness research is the role of timing. Clemens et al. (2012: 594), for instance, argue that when analysing aid effectiveness, it is crucial to bear in mind that different flows vary in the period it takes until their effects arrive. Following their argumentation (ibid.: 598), examples for aid that is assumed to have an early impact are investments in the transport, energy or agriculture system, as well as budget support. On the other hand, investments in the education or health system are typically considered to only show effects in the very long run (cf. Arndt et al. 2015: 9).

To tackle this issue, several studies look at various time intervals separately when analysing the impact of aid, such as Rajan and Subramanian (2008: 656) or Minoiu and Reddy (2010: 32). As different aid flows can vary widely regarding the period until positive effects may occur, it appears important to pay particular attention to the role of time when constructing estimation models. Therefore, this study follows the objective of differentiating between different possible timings of aid effects. This allows to gain a more complete picture of aid impacts on the one hand and, furthermore, provides insights into the period over which aid shows to have the highest impact.

---

[7] Another possibility of analysing the effect on social outcomes is to apply the HDI of the United Nations Development Programme (UNDP) as a composite statistic covering several different measures. This is done by Gomanee et al. (2005B: 301) or Kosack (2003: 7), for instance. McGillivray (1991: 1467), however, shows that the HDI is positively correlated with each of its components and concludes that it is not appropriate to apply as dependent variable. Therefore, this study focuses on the two areas health and education, as many studies of the aid literature consider either or both of them (see for instance Boone 1996: 303, Masud and Yontcheva 2005: 13-14 or Dreher et al. 2008: 297; 2010: 166).

4 Preliminary Empirical Analyses

To achieve these objectives, the approach of this study is as follows: The research objective of interest is the effect of aid on development, measured by economic growth, as well as indicators for education and health. With the general underlying assumption that aid effectiveness is significantly influenced by donor decisions, the aim is to subdivide aid flows by donors and to look at the respective impacts on the development measures separately. Besides a separation between bilateral and multilateral aid, this study also distinguishes between single bilateral donor countries based on the insights of the aid allocation literature, i.e. that there are considerable differences in motives of donor countries resulting in varying allocation patterns.

To determine the impact of aid on the chosen development indicators, the study applies both cross-sectional and dynamic panel data analyses. The focus, however, is on the latter one. Chapter 6 discusses the reasons why GMM methodology is the preferred approach. Regarding the observation period, the estimations consider the full coverage of available data, i.e. the period 1960-2014. In addition, a 25-year observation period covering 1990-2014 serves to determine differences in aid effectiveness after the end of the Cold War.

Before analysing the actual effect of aid from different donors, however, this chapter aims at providing evidence from a descriptive analysis. In a first step, main data sources, as well as definitions of the chosen parameters are presented. The second section then comprises the main part of the preliminary investigations. Based on the findings of the aid allocation literature, this analysis aims at determining differences in the way the chosen donors distribute aid. The objective here is to underpin the insight of the previous literature, and to verify if the main results, namely that major industrialised countries put a higher priority on own objectives than smaller Nordic bilateral donors, apply to the donors analysed in this study.

4.1 Data sources and definitions

To begin with, this section provides key definitions of the selected variables and presents the sources. A first issue to be addressed is the choice of the aid variables. The DAC database of the Organisation for Economic Co-operation and Development (OECD), as the most common source of the aid research, offers several different typed of aid measures. The three main types are total aid numbers, aid per capita of the recipient country population and aid as percent of the recipient country GDP (cf. OECD-DAC 2016). This study applies the latter measure, in line with most previous studies (cf. Rajan and Subramanian 2008: 651, Arndt et al. 2010: 8 or Clemens et al. 2012:

603). The straightforward reason for this choice is that several of the other explanatory variables also refer to GDP and, therefore, have a common reference point that facilitates interpretation.

A further aspect concerns the different elements of aid that one can consider for estimating aid effectiveness. One option is to exclude certain monetary flows, such as humanitarian aid or the repayments of assistance loans, as Headey (2008: 179), for instance, does. The objective of this study, however, is to capture the overall aid effects of each donor. Therefore, the subsequent estimations consider total aid flows, which comprise all grants and development loans with a grant element of at least 25% (cf. OECD-DAC 2016). This decision also corresponds to the approach of Rajan and Subramanian (2008: 662).

Now the focus is on the main aid variables of this study, i.e. those aim at determining differences among bilateral donors. Separating BA is achieved by forming groups of countries with a similar aid allocation, following the approach of Minoiu and Reddy (2010: 30). This procedure allows to observe sufficiently high aid flows and, thus, to potentially achieve better empirical results. In contrast to the separation strategy of Minoiu and Reddy (ibid.), however, this study aims at directly comparing one group of countries considered to allocate their aid effectively (from the recipient point of view), with another group of countries that are predominantly regarded as donors with an aid allocation oriented towards their own interests. The aim of this more direct comparison is to elaborate further in detail on the extent to which aid effectiveness can differ between different bilateral donors. According to Alesina and Dollar (2000: 42) and Berthélemy (2006A: 190-191), the four northern European countries Denmark, Finland, Norway and Sweden, as well as the Netherlands allocate aid strongly based on recipient needs and with a focus on development objectives.

For this reason, and because Minoiu and Reddy (2010: 33) observe a strong and significant positive relation between aid from these countries and growth in recipient countries, the choice of this study for the first group of countries, i.e. those with a "fair" allocation, is the same. The second group, however, differs from the decision of Minoiu and Reddy (2010: 30). As explained above, this group shall comprise countries with an allocation that presumably differs significantly from the one of group 1 donors (G1). Section 2.3.1. reveals that among such countries are France, Germany, Japan, the UK and the US. These countries form the second group of bilateral donors (G2). The table below gives a summary of the two groups of bilateral donors.

Appendix B1 shows the sources for all selected variables, distinguished by dependent variables, aid variables and the remaining control variables applied by the subsequent estimations. The respective analyses in section 5.1 and 5.2, moreover, explain which variables are applied for which estimation.

Table 1: *Group assignment of bilateral donors*

Group 1	Group 2
Denmark	France
Finland	Germany
The Netherlands	Japan
Norway	The United Kingdom
Sweden	The United States

Notes: Own illustration.

Appendix B2 presents a summary of the recipient countries considered in this study. The sample comprises nearly all countries that have received aid since the establishment of the DAC. A different approach would be to consider only a closer selection of aid recipients. Gomanee et al. (2005A: 1071), for instance, take into account only several LDCs in SSA, against the background that those countries have shown a particular low growth over the past decades. As the investigation of the subsequent section shows, however, such an approach would leave out major recipient countries of the analysed donor groups and, consequently, lead to a considerable bias of the eventual aid effectiveness.

4.2 Disaggregating aid – descriptive statistics

As some preliminary remarks to the empirical investigation of this study, this section illustrates differences in aid allocation of the chosen donor groups, based on the insights of the aid allocation literature. At this point, the term disaggregation requires a further explanation. As mentioned in section 2.3, aid flows can be separated in various ways. One option, for instance, is to distinguish between the purpose of aid that has been assigned by the donor. Several studies published over the last two decades apply such a procedure. One purpose behind this way of disaggregating aid can be to particularly analyse the effect of aid that is intended to increase the education level, such as Dreher et al. (2008: 300) do, or to only investigate those aid flows that are expected to have a short-term growth effect, as it is the approach of Clemens et al. (2012: 494). This thesis, however, investigates the total aggregated aid flows of the respectively considered donor. This has two main reasons.

Firstly, one can assume that aid under certain circumstances or specific types of aid flows are less effective than others. Kimura et al. (2012: 7-8), for instance, show that aid proliferation caused by excessive amounts of budget support or many projects executed by different donors can have a negative effect on growth. Consequently, if one considers only particular types of aid flows and leaves out others, it is possible that those kinds of aid that have no or a negative effect are not entering the final result. The aim of this

23

study, yet, is to determine differences between different donors. And because the aid allocation literature concludes that certain donors distribute higher shares of those types of aid that are regarded more effective than others, leaving out certain kinds of aid could distort the final result significantly.

The same argumentation applies to the use of such type of disaggregation applied by Clemens et al. (2012: 598-599), i.e. if one considers only the kinds of aid that are expected to have a positive effect in the short run. This procedure excludes all kinds of aid that are expected to show an impact in the long run or not at all. When comparing the effectiveness of different donors, the results of this procedure would be of very limited meaningfulness. Given the case that one finds a positive effect of the separated kinds of aid that should have an early impact and. Given that this positive impact would disappear completely when looking at the total aid numbers, one could argue that the share of the separated flows is not sufficiently high to enter the final result. Vice versa, the (potentially negative) influence of the formerly excluded flows could also be large enough to outweigh the other flows.

Secondly, excluding elements of aid that are assigned to certain sectors, such as to the health sector or to humanitarian needs, as Headey (2008: 169) or Clemens et al. (2012: 594) do, is not free from bias either. The rationale behind the strategy of these studies is these types of aid were originally not intended to affect growth and, thus, could be left out for a growth analysis. However, Bloom et al. (2004: 9-10) demonstrate that good health conditions have a significantly positive influence on growth. Therefore, there are no convincing arguments why aid assigned to the health sector, or even humanitarian aid, should not be considered when analysing the long-term effects of aid. Instead of dividing aid according to assigned purposes or sectors, this thesis attempts to capture the absolute flows of each donor and, thereby, to provide evidence for the overall differences amongst them. Figure 1 provides a first look at the total aid numbers of each donor in the course of aid history.

Looking at the development of aid payments over the past five decades, it becomes immediately apparent that donors of the first country group dominate the overall picture. During the 1960s, almost all aid labelled as ODA has been disbursed by the five countries of group 2. The major part of the payments over this period relates to US aid, accounting for almost 55% of the total aid flows spent in the 1960s.[8] With more than 12% of the aid disbursements in this period, France is also one of the first bilateral donors with large-scale aid programmes. During the 1970s, Germany, Japan and the UK additionally started to provide aid on a larger scale. Although the share of disbursements from other bilateral and multilateral donors has been growing constantly up to now, the

---

[8] Appendix C1 provides information about the aid payments of each of the investigated donor in five year averages.

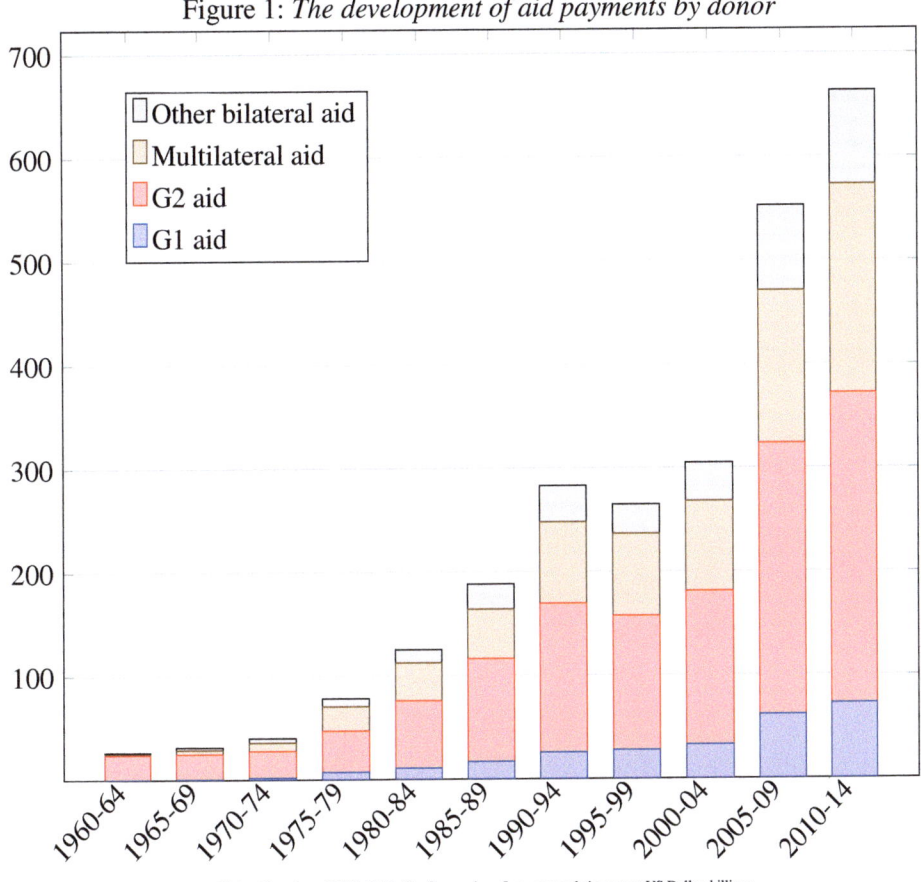

Figure 1: *The development of aid payments by donor*

share of G2 countries in total aid disbursements was still 45% over the period 2010-2014 and almost USD 300 billion in total.

Compared to these numbers, G1 countries account for a much lower proportion of total aid flows. However, considering that all donors in this group are relatively small countries by population, they are among the donors with the highest aid per capita payments. In the mid-1970s, Sweden and the Netherlands started larger aid programmes. In the early 1980s, furthermore, Denmark and Norway essentially extended their aid disbursements. Up to the present, Finland has been a relatively small donor compared to the other countries of this group. Only during the late 2000s, Finland started to increase its aid funds significantly. Over the past five years of the observation period (2010-2014), G1 countries almost accounted for almost a quarter of the aid disbursed by G2, with total disbursements of more than USD 72 billion. Considering the ratio between the aid numbers of the two groups, one can conclude about a first shortcoming of measuring the effect of aggregated aid, or aggregated bilateral aid. Given that the allocation of aid and, consequently, the resulting effectiveness differs between the two donor groups, it is easy to picture that potentially positive effects of a small G1 donors could be alleviated by those of just one big G2 country. This is a further reason why investigating aid effectiveness of different donors separately could provide additional insights.

A similar amount of aid to that of G1 is added by the remaining bilateral donors of the DAC.[9] Multilateral donors also disburse a considerable share of aid which has sharply been increasing over the past decades. As mentioned before, several studies show that multilateral aid had worked better over regarding the effect on growth, such as Burnside and Dollar (2000: 863) or Headey (2008: 170). One consequence of such findings could be that one can observe a significant increase in the share of multilateral aid over the past years (as figure 1 shows).

After looking at the total aid numbers divided by donor, a further view on allocation patterns of individual donors aims at providing first evidence for the divergence in aid effectiveness between different donors. Since one of the main targets of this study is to analyse the differences amongst bilateral donors, the following overview (table 2) focuses on the two selected country groups. The table shows the pattern of aid allocation while considering the ten recipient countries with the highest amounts of aid received from the two groups respectively. In doing so, it distinguishes between the two periods 1960-1989 and 1990-2014 with the purpose of capturing changes between the pre- and post-Cold War era. Moreover, infant mortality and income per capita, two of the major indicators for measuring development in the aid effectiveness literature, are included for each recipient country and the two periods, to enable a simplified illustration of differences in the consideration of recipient needs.

When comparing the differences between the two periods, it firstly becomes apparent that both donor groups diversify aid more broadly after the end of the Cold War. Whereas G1 (G2) allocated approximately 47% (36%) of the total aid budget to the first five recipient countries in the period 1960-1989, the respective shares decrease to 31% (23%) in the period afterwards. This could have several reasons. One possibility is that donors have expanded their aid portfolio and established relations with more recipient countries over the time. One could also explain this by drawing on those findings of the aid allocation literature that refer to changes in donor motives after the end of the Cold War, as outlined in section 2.3.1. Thus, the importance of political relations with individual recipient countries could have decreased after the reduction of global tensions. Other motives, such as the quality of the recipients' governance and policy environments, could in turn have increased. This reasoning would be in line with the results of Dollar and Levin (2006: 2042). Their estimations show an increasing role

---

[9]It is worth mentioning that there are several other bilateral donors that are not part of the DAC. The disbursements of some of them are also listed in the OECD-DAC (2016) database. However, those of other important donors, such as China, are still not reported. For this reason, Figure 1 refers to bilateral donors that are part of the DAC only. For further information, Dreher et al. (2011), for instance, investigate the aid allocation of those donor countries that have recently emerged and which are already listed in OECD-DAC.

Table 2: *Aid allocation of bilateral donor groups*

	Group 1 Aid				Group 2 Aid		
			1960-1989				
Recipient	Aid received (as percentage)	GDP per capita (constant USD)	Infant Mortality (per 1000 births)	Recipient	Aid received (as percentage)	GDP per capita (constant USD)	Infant Mortality (per 1000 births)
Tanzania	14.28%	475.08	120.03	Israel	8.79%	14820.51	15.31
India	12.59%	399.56	127.98	India	8.59%	399.56	127.98
Bangladesh	7.44%	371.65	140.29	Egypt, Arab Rep.	8.34%	1075.31	136.11
Indonesia	6.49%	910.50	100.78	Indonesia	5.78%	910.50	100.78
Kenya	6.32%	751.22	82.16	Pakistan	4.64%	505.97	135.32
Mozambique	5.57%	158.75	175.95	Bangladesh	3.79%	371.65	140.29
Zambia	4.44%	1391.76	106.04	Philippines	3.09%	1393.74	54.57
Sri Lanka	3.38%	827.08	45.24	Turkey	2.91%	4587.36	108.43
Pakistan	2.79%	505.97	135.32	China	2.49%	319.27	55.54
Ethiopia	2.69%	216.50	138.89	Korea, Rep.	2.41%	3389.76	30.99
			1990 - 2014				
Tanzania	9.48%	590.44	69.04	Egypt, Arab Rep.	5.39%	2124.61	36.37
Mozambique	7.71%	309.04	105.59	China	5.12%	2768.01	25.52
Uganda	4.79%	476.53	76.30	India	4.76%	996.81	61.79
Bangladesh	4.56%	601.66	60.10	Nigeria	4.18%	1726.06	102.19
Zambia	4.39%	1149.42	81.14	Pakistan	3.61%	923.91	84.88
Ethiopia	3.81%	258.53	79.45	Indonesia	3.10%	2560.52	39.08
Kenya	3.31%	921.34	57.12	Ethiopia	3.10%	258.53	79.45
Ghana	2.99%	1123.29	60.95	Congo, Dem. Rep.	2.88%	349.78	100.02
Nicaragua	2.96%	1378.95	31.50	Tanzania	2.60%	590.44	69.04
Congo, Dem. Rep.	2.92%	349.78	100.02	Kenya	2.58%	921.34	57.12

Notes: Data from OECD-DAC and WDI. The table shows only the recipient countries of the sample (see Appendix B1). Additional countries with high aid receipts might be omitted.

of variables measuring good recipient policies for explaining the allocation pattern of bilateral donors after 1989.

Focusing on the temporal changes in the G1 aid allocation, one can observe that there are no major changes regarding the choice of recipient countries. Out of the ten countries that received the highest amounts of aid by these donors before 1990, six remain among the key recipients during the second period. Yet, one can notice one peculiarity of the G1 allocation: Countries in SSA seem to have a particularly high role among their recipient countries. Five of the recipients during the first period, and even seven during the second period are located in this area. This comprehensive priority of G1 countries for allocating aid towards SSA, moreover, can be recognised when looking at each of the donor separately.[10] Alesina and Dollar (2000: 42-44) also find that Scandinavian donors tend to spend high amounts of aid to African recipient countries, and additionally show that this choice of allocation is not motivated by political interest. One can rather assume that a high need for further development in these countries drives their choice. Countries in SSA are both before and as from 1990 among the countries with the lowest per capita income and the highest infant mortality, as table 2 demonstrates.

The allocation of G2 donors shows quite a different picture. Countries that exhibit a relatively high level of development are not only among the donors with the largest aid receipts before 1990, but also during the post-Cold War period. Because each of the donors of this group shows a very characteristic allocation pattern, it is worth taking a closer look at the individual allocation patterns (appendix C3), instead of discussing the group-comprehensive numbers at this point. In this way, one can conclude about the

---

[10]To provide more accurate information, appendix C2 and C3 additionally shows the aid allocation of each bilateral donor of the two groups separately.

individual power-political and geographical interest of the donors discussed in section 2.3.1. It is striking, for instance, that Israel is the country with by far the highest US aid receipts in the period before 1990 (13,5%) and still the second most important recipient in the period afterwards, whereas it is not among the top recipients of neither of the other G2 donors over the post-Cold War period, and only among those of Germany in the period until 1989. Other countries in this region, such as Egypt, Turkey or Jordan, are also among the countries with the highest shares of US aid.

The focus of US aid to those countries of the MENA region that are considered to have pro-Western regimes is in line with the findings of Harrigan and Wang (2011: 1288). Based on an analysis of the main factors for explaining the allocation pattern of several bilateral and multilateral donors, they show that US aid is highly correlated with geo-political interests. With Israel and Egypt being among the key recipients as well, Germany seems to allocate aid in a very similar pattern to the US. Moreover, it is striking that China has received the highest share of German aid during the second period. Corresponding to this, Berthélemy (2006A) shows that German aid is moderately and significantly correlated with the German trade pattern. Alesina and Dollar (2000: 46), moreover find that German aid is highly correlated with its UN voting pattern. These interactions could explain, amongst other reasons, why a larger share of German and US aid is allocated to more advanced countries rather than to those with high humanitarian or development needs.

Focusing on the recipients of Japanese aid, appendix C3 shows that countries in East Asia, such as the Philippines or Indonesia, prove to dominate the allocation picture regardless of the period. Schraeder et al. (300) point out that the recipient choice of Japan is primarily based on its trade interests and geo-economic interest. This conclusion could be one cause for the observed concentration of Japanese aid to the East Asian region. Turning towards the remaining two donors of G2, it becomes apparent that both French and UK aid has largely been directed to former colonies. Examples for these are India, Kenya or Bangladesh in the case of the UK, and the francophone-African countries Morocco, Algeria, Senegal, Cameroon and Côte d'Ivoire in the case of France. As discussed in section 2.3.1, there are several studies that find a strong influence of former colonial ties on the aid allocation of major donors. Some argue that this points towards the high importance of aid as an instrument for promoting strategic donor interest, such as Alesina and Dollar (2000: 55). On the other hand, as mentioned earlier in this section, one can also observe that each of the G2 donors increasingly dispersed aid over the second period. Furthermore, several countries with a relatively low per capita income and a relatively high infant mortality rate are added to their allocation after the end of the Cold War, e.g. Tanzania or Kenya.

To sum up the main points of this section, three main insights shall be highlighted:

First, the amount of aid payments of the two defined donor groups varies significantly. Looking at the whole observation period, G1 donors spend only a small share of aid compared to donors of G2. Second, a glance at the aid allocation points towards differences between the two donor groups, which one can potentially explain with the insights of the aid allocation literature – namely that the motives for allocating aid differs significantly between the two groups. Third, it becomes apparent that both donors have changed their aid allocation when looking at the pre- and post-1989 periods. However, these changes appear to be only moderate.

The first empirical analyses complete the basic framework and provide further reasons to assume that there are donor-specific differences in aid effectiveness, which might vary to an extent that is quantitative measurable.

5 A first approximation: Cross-Country Evidence

Taking together the findings of the existing literature that are presented in chapter 2 plus the observations of the previous section, this chapter now attempts to measure aid effectiveness based on a donor-related disaggregation. A cross-sectional analysis (in the following also termed cross-country analysis) forms the starting point for this purpose. As previously stated in section 2.1, early studies of the aid research literature already analyse the relationship between aid and growth based on cross-sectional data in the 1970s. Since then, it has remained an essential procedure in the research field, and has experienced increased application over the past years. Rajan and Subramanian (2008: 645-647), Chong et al. (2009: 66-70), Arndt et al. (2010:7-8, 2015A:9-10) as well as Minoiu and Reddy (2010: 31-35) among others adopt a detailed OLS estimation based on cross-country data before running dynamic panel data analyses. However, there are several reasons why a dynamic panel analysis should be the preferred approach - as outlined in the following chapter. Therefore, this preliminary analysis serves as a first approximation with the aim of providing a first impression of the relation between aid and the chosen final outcomes, distinguished by the different donors.

The analysis starts with an investigation of the impact on growth as the most common indicator for aid effectiveness. It then addresses the effects on the two social success indicators infant mortality and primary enrolment rate as measures for health and educational quality. While the main regressions observe averages over the full period 1960-2014 with an aid horizon of 1960-1990 and the observation period 1990-2014 of the indicator, a third section includes variations of observation periods with the purpose of determining quantitative changes of the aid effect after the Cold War and, by doing so, provides a first robustness test for the estimations of the main period.

5.1 The effect on growth

As section 2.1 indicates, and as Doucouliagos und Paldam (2009:441-445) discuss in more detail, results of previous aid effectiveness studies are highly sensitive to the methodological approach and the applied regression specification, particularly the choice of explanatory variables. Differences in empirical procedure are in fact one of the main reasons for divergent conclusions within the aid literature. Temple (2010: 4449) addresses this issue and states that a favourable approach is to build on existing work, in order to increase coherence and comparability of the empirical findings in the long run. The strategy of this study, therefore, is to apply specifications of existing studies that are considered well-elaborated and highly influential on recent research.

Additionally, the purpose in this context is to draw on those studies that find no positive effect of aggregated aid. The intention behind this choice is that insights, given that one finds a positive effect of certain donor countries while aggregated aid remains ineffective, are more valuable than they would be with total aid already having a significantly positive effect. Because of different causalities between aid and growth, and aid and social outcomes, different specifications are needed respectively. For the aid-growth analysis, regressions of this study take up the specification of Rajan and Subramanian (2008: 646). Several studies published in recent years, for instance both Clemens et al. (2012: 590-591) and Arndt et al. (2010: 6), point to the good elaboration and great influence of the study by Rajan and Subramanian (2008) and build on its specifications.

The original approach of Rajan and Subramanian (2008)[11] includes analyses on the basis of both cross-section (650-657) and panel data (657-659) methodology over the period 1960-2000. This comprises variations of observation periods, estimators and the type of aid, e.g. economic aid or those flows assigned to social areas (656). Moreover, the authors address the before-mentioned issue of the choice of explanatory variables and, therefore, apply an intersection of the variables of four previous influential studies. In this way, they obtain the following control variables for measuring other impacts on growth in recipient countries apart aid: The initial level of per capita income, institutional quality, financial depth, revolutions, ethnic fractionalisation, trade policy, the level of inflation and budget balance to GDP. Additionally, they introduce extreme climatic conditions as a measure for geography and life expectancy as a measure for health conditions (646). It should be noted once again that the Rajan and Subramanian (2008: 660) do not find any significant positive effect of aid in neither of their estimations.

The following analysis investigates the effect of the development assistance per GDP

---

[11]The following page numbers in this paragraph, in parentheses, refer to the study of Rajan and Subramanian (2008).

ratio as the explanatory variable of interest. The dependent variable is the annual GDP growth per capita in the recipient country. The observation period is extended to the full available sample 1960-2014. In contrast to previous studies that build on the work of Rajan and Subramanian (2008), such as Arndt et al. (2010: 14-15) or Minoiu and Reddy (2010: 32), the aim of this thesis is to stick to the original specification as close as possible. The basic purpose of this is to avoid altering the original results by changing variables and, thus, to gain the maximum explanatory power of diverging findings after separating the donors.

Some modifications of the original specification nevertheless have to be made: First, the two variables ethnic fractionalisation and financial depth to GDP are left out. The two ratios financial depth to GDP and budget balance to GDP are highly correlated, as one reason. Moreover, the two omitted variables appear to be insignificant across all the estimations, including the original ones of Rajan and Subramanian (2008). Arndt et al. (2010: 14) note this shortcoming as well and conclude that leaving out these variables is the preferred procedure. Second, the two variables institutional quality and revolutions are replaced by variables with an equal meaning and equal or higher significance for the reasons of data availability and topicality. The average number of revolutions per year in Rajan and Subramanian (2008: 646) as a measure of political stability is replaced by the average annual number of politically motivated violence from the Integrated Network for Societal Conflict Research (INSCR) database. Institutional quality, included in the original only until the year 1995, is in this study represented by a measure of economic freedom that includes several quality indicators of legal, economic, regulation, governmental and monetary institutions.

Both replacement variables, especially the measure for institutional quality, prove to by higher in significance than the original ones and show the right expected sign. Third, Rajan and Subramanian (2008: 662) consider only the first five years of each observation period for the variables inflation and budget balances. Because the cross-section part of this study analyses observation periods of more than 20 years, it is unlikely that periods of five years represent the economic situation of the individual recipient countries. For a better economic interpretation, this study applies the average inflation rates, as well as the ration of budget balance to GDP over the total observation periods. The remaining explanatory variables are identical to the original specification, with time periods extended to the present. Appendix B1 outlines the variables for the aid-growth analysis, their sources, as well as detailed explanations.

For the purpose of measuring differences in aid effectiveness among donors, total aid numbers are disaggregated in three different ways: One regression separates total aid into the payments of bilateral and multilateral donors. The other two equations divide aid numbers into those of either of the two groups of bilateral countries, as the variable of direct interest, and the aid payments of all other donors, e.g. total aid minus the payments of only the respective group, as a further variable. The following equations show the coefficients that are estimated to answer the research questions:

$$\Delta y_i = \beta_0 + \alpha_{ba}ba_i + \alpha_{ma}ma_i + \sum_{j=1}^{k} \gamma_j x_{ji} + \varepsilon_i \tag{1}$$

$$\Delta y_i = \beta_0 + \alpha_1 G1_i + \alpha_{n1} n\_G1_i + \sum_{j=1}^{k} \gamma_j x_{ji} + \varepsilon_i \tag{2}$$

$$\Delta y_i = \beta_0 + \alpha_2 G2_i + \alpha_{n2} n\_G2_i + \sum_{j=1}^{k} \gamma_j x_{ji} + \varepsilon_i \tag{3}$$

where Δy_i denotes the average GDP growth per capita in the recipient country i. The explanatory variables of interest are ba_i (ma_i) representing aid payments from bilateral (multilateral) donors to country i in equation (1), as well as $G1_i$ and $G2_i$ denoting the aid payments of the two bilateral donor groups to recipient country i in equations (2) and (3). The respective coefficients for measuring the interaction between the different aid flows and economic growth of recipient countries are α_{ba}, α_{ma}, α_1 and α_2. The latter two equations include the aid amounts of all other donors N_G1_1 and N_G2_1 with their coefficients N_G1_i and N_G2_i. The term n_G1_1, for instance, represents the difference between aid paid by all other donors minus aid from the five bilateral donors countries of group 1. In all the equations, $\sum_{j=1}^{k} \gamma_j x_{ji}$ denotes the remaining explanatory variables x that might affect growth and their coefficients γ_j. Furthermore, β_0 represents a constant and ε_i is the error term.

The approach of including the amount of all remaining donors besides the aid flows of the donor group as the explanatory variable of interest is similar to the one of Minoiu and Reddy (2010: 30). Rajan and Subramanian (2008: 656), in contrast to this, do only include the aid flows of the five donor countries they want to inspect into their regressions. Aid flows of the remaining donors, however, is a decisive variable that should not be omitted. As we have seen in section 4.2, the Scandinavian donors only account for a small share of total aid flows. However, if one considers that aid accounts for a relatively high proportion of the domestic GDP in some developing countries, it appears necessary to consider aid flows as a whole in each estimation. Consequently, a separation of the aid flows belonging to only one donor or a group of donors should always be complemented with the aid flows of all other donors that are not included in the aid variable of interest. The table below presents the first estimations of the aid-growth relationship based on OLS cross-country regressions.

The first column, corresponding to equation (1), shows the separation between bilateral and multilateral aid. The coefficients for both BA and MA are insignificant. Whereas

Table 3: *OLS cross-sectional estimations: Aid and growth*

	Dependent variable: Average annual growth rate in 1990-2014		
	(1)	(2)	(3)
BA 1960-1999	3.455		
	(8.387)		
MA 1960-1999	-18.46		
	(17.24)		
G1 aid 1960-1999		49.39**	
		(22.25)	
Non G1 aid 1960-1999		-15.05***	
		(5.424)	
G2 aid 1960-1999			-27.41**
			(12.17)
Non G2 aid 1960-1999			1.725
			(5.024)
Initial Income	-0.729**	-0.733**	-0.762**
	(0.358)	(0.339)	(0.339)
Initial life expectancy	2.568	1.720	2.359
	(2.086)	(1.965)	(1.905)
Institutional quality	0.657**	0.785***	0.745***
	(0.265)	(0.262)	(0.243)
Geography	0.450*	0.491**	0.479**
	(0.242)	(0.228)	(0.232)
Budget balance	0.0178	0.0215	0.00933
	(0.0421)	(0.0364)	(0.0396)
Political instability	0.124	0.103	0.0823
	(0.105)	(0.0988)	(0.102)
Initial policy	-0.297	-0.508	-0.423
	(0.385)	(0.373)	(0.366)
Inflation	-0.00214***	-0.00232***	-0.00226***
	(0.000504)	(0.000400)	(0.000507)
Constant	-6.419	-3.205	-5.359
	(6.924)	(6.064)	(6.321)
Observations	73	73	73
R-squared	0.441	0.507	0.474

Sources: Author's calculations.
Notes: The dependent variable is the average annual growth rate of GDP per capita during the period 1990-2014. Robust standard errors in parentheses. For descriptions of the variables and their sources, see appendix B1. ***, ** and * denote statistical significance at the 1%, 5%, and 10% level respectively.

the coefficient for BA is weakly positive, the sign MA appears to be even negative. The results that both MA and BA show to have no significant effect on growth is in line with the original findings of Rajan and Subramanian (2008: 656). However, they are strongly in contrast to the conclusions of the aid allocation literature, i.e. that multilateral agencies put a higher emphasis on needs and good policies of recipient countries, as well as to other previous findings of the aid-growth literature, such as (Headey 2008: 170), who finds effectiveness of MA to be significantly higher than the one of BA.

Turning to the main variables of interest, namely the influence of the two bilateral donor groups, the results from this first approximation are quite clear. Both of their coefficients are significant on a 5% level and different from zero, but vary in sign. Whereas the coefficient for G1 aid is positive and accounts for almost 50, the respective estimation for G2 indicates that aid flows effect growth negatively, however, to only nearly half of the extent. These results suggest that an additional percentage point of aid per GDP from G1 donors during the period 1960-1999 is associated with an increase in GDP per capita in recipient countries of about half a percentage point in 1990-2014. Figure 2(a) displays this correlation. The coefficient for G2 donors, on the other hand, indicates that increases in aid of about one percentage points implicate a decrease in GDP of about 0.27 percentage points. Combining the results for the coefficients of the two groups, this first insight corresponds to the findings of Minoiu and Reddy (2010: 33). In a first estimation, they find an increase in GDP growth of more than one percentage point when considering only G1 donors. After including five further bilateral donors into the aid variable, among them France and the United Kingdom, the coefficient sharply decreases to around 0.15 percentage points.

Figure 2: *Conditional relationships between aid and growth*

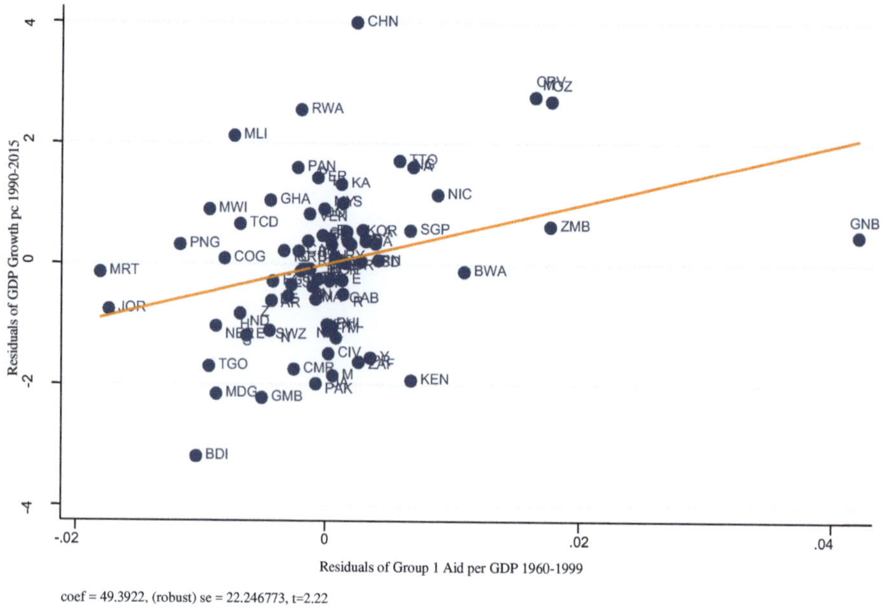

coef = 49.3922, (robust) se = 22.246773, t=2.22

(a) Growth and group 1 aid

coef = -27.4120, (robust) se = 12.172768, t=-2.25

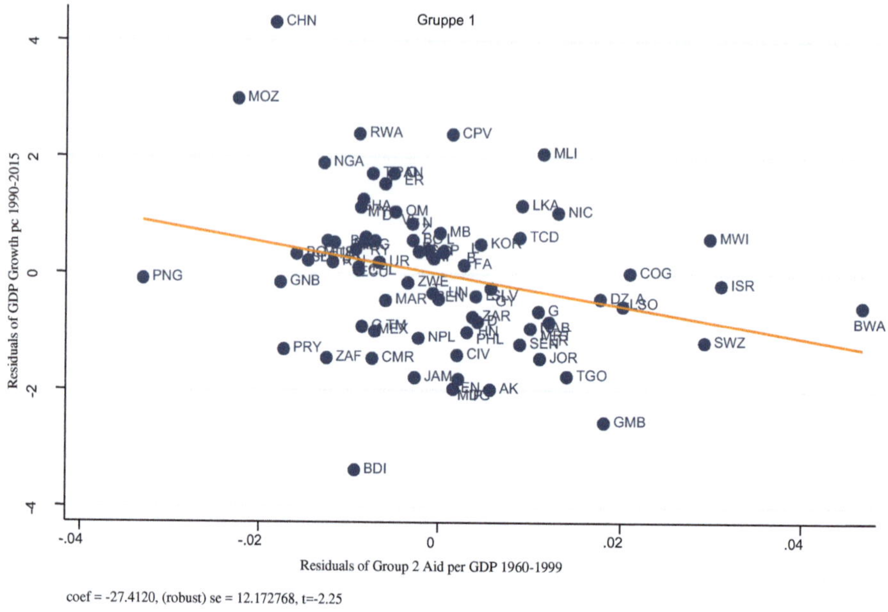

(b) Growth and group 2 aid

Notes: The scatter plots show the correlation between average GDP growth per capita in recipient countries for 1990-2015 and aid flows of group 1 donors (a) as well as group 2 donors (b) for 1960-1999, conditional on all the covariates. The slope of the lines reflect the coefficient on aid in the OLS regressions in columns 2 and 3 of table 3. Abbreviations of the groups/recipient countries can be found in Appendix B1.

Considering the clear difference between the two donor groups and, additionally, recalling that G2 donors account for a large share of total aid numbers, it becomes evident that it is necessary to include the two contrasting variables n_G1_1 and n_G2_1 into the regressions. The coefficient of all aid except that from G1 donors in the second column, for instance, is highly significant and suggests that the aid of all non-group 1 donors decreases growth in recipient countries moderately. To reinforce the argument that regressions should include remaining aid as an additional variable, appendix D1 shows the estimates for identical regressions to the second and third column of figure 1 with the only difference that the variables n_G1_1 and n_G2_1 are left out. After omitting the variable for the (large) remaining aid flows and, thus, after not considering the effect of the remaining aid, the coefficient of group 1 aid considerably decreases to 23.94 and loses significance.

As stated at the beginning of this chapter, however, these results are only intended to be a first indication for the estimation. The OLS-based cross-section procedure lacks important empirical characteristics, as discussed at the beginning of the following chapter. For this reason, the results shall not be interpreted as hard evidence, but rather as initial pointers of the measurements. A detailed discussion of the findings follows the dynamic panel data analysis. This also includes further explanations on the negative parameters of aid variables, as these require careful interpretation.

5.2 The effect on social indicators

After having provided a first impression of quantitative differences between the effects on growth as the common research object within the literature, the focus is now directed towards the achievements of development aid regarding particular social objectives. This follows from the fact that there is very little empirical evidence on how aid appears to impact social indicators. As it becomes apparent in appendix A, several MDGs as well as newly formed SDGs fall into the fields of health on education. Because of good data availability in these areas, this study attempts to elaborate on one key indicator for each of them. Since the focus of analysis is not an economic variable any longer, but on indicators in social areas, different covariates to the estimates in the previous section are needed. Similar to the approach of the aid-growth analysis in the subsequent section, estimations for this part likewise build on existing regression specifications. Masud and Yontcheva (2005: 13-14) provide a first point of reference for measuring aid effects on both indicators for educational and health quality. In two separate regressions, they determine the impact on infant mortality and adult illiteracy rate and, in doing so, distinguish between the effects of BA and aid from NGO donors.

The two original specifications of Masud and Yontcheva (ibid.) cover the same set of covariates, except that the infant mortality regression includes two additional variables.

The common control variables of both estimations that are supposed to effect social development are urbanisation rate, poverty headcount ratio, population growth rate, income per capita, the level of governance as well as a dummy variable indicating whether a recipient country is supported by a structural adjustment programme of the International Monetary Fund (IMF) or not. The two additional variables of the infant mortality regression are the agricultural value added by worker and female illiteracy (cf. Masud and Yontcheva 2005: 13). Based on fixed and random effect panel data analyses, the authors find that the impact of NGO aid on infant mortality appears to be significantly, but only moderately negative. A negative sign in this case means that NGO aid helps to reduce infant mortality. In contrast, BA does not show to reduce infant mortality in the original regressions (ibid.). Regarding the impact on the illiteracy rate in recipient countries, the authors find no positive impact of neither NGO nor bilateral aid.

Once again, the aim is to change the original specifications as little as possible. The only explanatory variable that is removed is the IMF dummy. Because the initial objective of including this dummy is to test for the effectiveness of IMF structural programmes (cf. Masud and Yontcheva 2005: 18), it can be dropped for the estimations of this study without misgivings about the explanatory power of the variable set. The remaining deviations from the original specifications are only minor. The variable for institutional variable is from a different source, as discussed in the previous section. Aid variables, as well as health and education expenditures are included as ratios to GDP and not defined per capita like in the original. Finally, the covariate of female illiteracy rate is replaced by female literacy rate. This however, affects only the sign of the variable.

A further change to Masud and Yontcheva (2005: 14) concerns the dependent variable for measuring educational quality. Instead of the rate of adult illiteracy like in the original, this study considers the primary completion rate for the education regressions. This decision is based on significantly better data quality of the latter indicator, which especially applies for the following panel data analysis. Concerning the observation period of the subsequent chapter, which comprises eleven five-year periods, the rate primary completion of the World Development Indicators (WDI) has almost twice as many observation compared to the rate of adult illiteracy. Moreover, Dreher et al. (2008: 299) also apply primary completion for their analysis of the effects of education aid on educational quality as the dependent variable of choice, while using a very similar set of explanatory variables. For the sake of comparability between the cross-sectional and the panel data investigations, primary completion shall also be the dependent variable in this section. Next, political instability is added as an additional covariate to both the regressions. This variable, also included in the growth regressions, proved to have a significant impact with the expected sign in several of the social indicators estimations as well. Because political conflicts, such as civil wars as a more severe case, often have a negative impact on living conditions (cf. Pedersen 2002: 181-183), the introduced measure is supposed to be a meaningful supplement to the regressions.

The observation period for the following estimations is, equal to the previous section, 1960-2014 with an aid horizon 1960-1999 and 1990-2014 for the two dependent variables. The regression equations for separating aid are also identical to the three equations (1) – (3) of the growth part, with the exception that the dependent variables on the left-hand side are now the average annual rate of infant mortality as the indicator for health and the average annual primary completion rate representing educational quality. The analysis starts with the findings of the infant mortality estimations and then turns to the effects on primary completion. The table below shows the results of the first cross-sectional analysis. Again, the first column distinguishes between MA and BA effects, whereas the latter two separate G1 and G2 from the total aid flows.

Table 4: *OLS cross-sectional estimations: Aid and infant mortality*

	Dependent variable: Decrease in infant mortality between 1990 and 2014		
	(1)	(2)	(3)
BA 1960-1999	**0.593**		
	(1.619)		
MA 1960-1999	**-0.776**		
	(3.068)		
G1 aid 1960-1999		**-2.861**	
		(2.361)	
Non G1 aid 1960-1999		0.973	
		(1.031)	
G2 aid 1960-1999			**3.116**
			(1.892)
Non G2 aid 1960-1999			-0.605
			(0.597)
Health expenditure	0.00867	0.00494	0.00160
	(0.0197)	(0.0196)	(0.0191)
Urbanisation	-0.0800*	-0.0680	-0.0729
	(0.0469)	(0.0473)	(0.0462)
Rural development	-0.0106	-0.00267	0.000453
	(0.0377)	(0.0400)	(0.0385)
Initial income	0.0672*	0.0640*	0.0630*
	(0.0376)	(0.0360)	(0.0358)
Poverty	0.0274	0.0281	0.0205
	(0.0274)	(0.0278)	(0.0272)
Population growth	0.0389	0.0356	0.0289
	(0.0300)	(0.0305)	(0.0290)
Institutional Quality	0.00659	0.00597	-0.00654
	(0.0401)	(0.0416)	(0.0421)
Political Instability	-0.00579	-0.00321	0.000289
	(0.0131)	(0.0136)	(0.0129)
Female literacy	-0.000636	2.73e-05	8.92e-06
	(0.00152)	(0.00149)	(0.00147)
Constant	-0.791	-0.929*	-0.831
	(0.501)	(0.528)	(0.505)
Observations	72	72	72
R-squared	0.169	0.191	0.219

Sources: Author's calculations.
Notes: The dependent variable is the decrease rate of infant mortality between the years 1990 and the 2014. Robust standard errors in parentheses. For descriptions of the variables and their sources, see appendix B1.
***, ** and * denote statistical significance at the 1%, 5%, and 10% level respectively.

Let us now proceed to the effects on the level of education. What first strikes when looking at the results of table 4 is that across all three estimations, including the explanatory variables of interest in the first six rows, there are hardly significant coefficients compared to the growth cross-sectional part. Because this feature changes clearly in the subsequent panel data analyses, it should be noted before interpreting the findings in detail that a cross-sectional approach might not be appropriate for these specifications. However, despite missing significances, a first difference between the donors becomes apparent. As mentioned above, a negative sign of a coefficient implicates that the respective determinant decreases infant mortality. This can be observed for multilateral and G1 aid, which would (with significant coefficients) be indicating that these two donors achieve the goal of reducing infant mortality, whereas the coefficients for bilateral and G2 aid suggest that the opposite. Yet, the first results provide no reasons for a more detailed discussion.

Table 5: *OLS cross-sectional estimations: Aid and primary completion*

	Dependent variable: Increase in primary completion between 1990 and 2014		
	(1)	(2)	(3)
BA 1960-1999	-2.752		
	(3.072)		
MA 1960-1999	5.266		
	(5.453)		
G1 aid 1960-1999		0.0894	
		(5.908)	
Non G1 aid 1960-1999		0.417	
		(1.755)	
G2 aid 1960-1999			0.702
			(3.379)
Non G2 aid 1960-1999			0.231
			(1.963)
Health expenditure	-0.0525**	-0.0618***	-0.0621***
	(0.0244)	(0.0218)	(0.0215)
Urbanisation	0.0701	0.0423	0.0413
	(0.131)	(0.119)	(0.115)
Initial income	-0.237**	-0.229**	-0.229**
	(0.0937)	(0.0936)	(0.0929)
Poverty	0.0133	0.000933	-0.000912
	(0.0567)	(0.0538)	(0.0554)
Poverty	0.125	0.143	0.143
	(0.111)	(0.107)	(0.105)
Institutional Quality	-0.0480	-0.0604	-0.0618
	(0.0738)	(0.0674)	(0.0691)
Political Instability	-0.124**	-0.125**	-0.124**
	(0.0546)	(0.0561)	(0.0558)
Constant	2.277**	2.404**	2.418**
	(1.074)	(0.992)	(0.988)
Observations	50	50	50
R-squared	0.576	0.567	0.567

Sources: Author's calculations.
Notes: The dependent variable is the increase rate of primary completion between the years 1990 and the 2014. Robust standard errors in parentheses. For descriptions of the variables and their sources, see appendix B1.
***, ** and * denote statistical significance at the 1%, 5%, and 10% level respectively.

The same applies for the results of the primary completion estimations shown in table 5. While three of the covariates are significant, one of them does not show the expected sign. Since now the dependent variable is the increase rate in primary completion over the observation period, a negative sign of the coefficients indicates that the corresponding variables are negatively correlated with development of educational systems. This is plausible for the influence of political instability, but not for health expenditure. For this reason alone, the results of this cross-sectional study shall not be discussed as concrete evidence. Regarding the negative coefficient initial income, one could argue that it is the expected sign with the interpretation that higher levels of GDP per capita at the beginning of the observation period are followed by weaker increases of educational quality due to an already higher initial value. Turning to the aid variables, and once more ignoring the lack of significance, MA again appears to be more effective in reaching development goals than BA. Regarding the two donor groups, this first approximation indicates that neither of their aid helps to improve the level of education. However, it shall once again be emphasised that this first cross-sectional evidence, particularly the social indicators analysis, does not provide a broad basis for detailed discussion.

5.3 Post-Cold War changes

Up to now, all the estimations have covered the full observation period 1960-2014. Because the aid allocation literature suggests that donor motives have changed since the end of the Cold War and, this section aims at providing a first insight on how the effectiveness of aid quantitatively changes after the year 1989. The strategy for achieving this objective is to analyse aid effects over three different 20-year observation periods – the first lying entirely inside the Cold War period (1970-1989), the second overlapping the periods before and after the Cold War (1980-1999) and the third only covering years after the end of the Cold War (1990-2009). To provide a first impression of these time-related changes, the focus within the scope of the cross-sectional part is limited to the impacts of growth. Respective analyses of the two social indicators follow in the next chapter. For reasons of comparability, the growth horizon of 15 years is chosen in such a way that growth periods follow the 20-year aid periods with the same lag. In this way, one obtains four different estimations, each including the three regressions that differentiate between donors, as well as the same specifications as in table 3. Their results are listed in table 6, which refers to the procedure of Rajan and Subramanian (2008: 656) with, firstly, an extended period to observe the post-Cold War effects and, secondly, regressions that differ between donor groups and respective differences to total aid numbers.

Table 6: *First evidence of post-Cold War changes in aid effectiveness*

| | | Donor | Growth Horizon: 15 years | |
			1990-2005	2000-2015
Aid Horizon: 20 years	1970-1990	G1 aid	22.47* (11.33)	-
		G2 aid	-17.05 (14.99)	-
		BA/ MA	-9.73/ -1.783 (7.720)/ (22.89)	-
	1980-2000	G1 aid	42.66** (16.72)	31.05* (16.03)
		G2 aid	-20.24 (13.37)	-20.55 (13.68)
		BA/ MA	-4.675/ 2.199 (9.71)/ (17.69)	9.125/ -10.09 (7.368)/ (11.99)
	1990-2010	G1 aid	-	66.06*** (18.78)
		G2 aid	-	-5.286 (13.21)
		BA/ MA	-	2.629/ -0.729 (9.130)/ (14.38)

Sources: Author's calculations.
Notes: The dependent variable is the average GDP growth rate during the two periods 1990-2005 and 2000-2015. Only coefficients of the explanatory variables of interest are reported, appendices D2-D5 show the full estimations. Robust standard errors in parentheses. For descriptions of the variables and their sources, see appendix B1. ***, ** and * denote statistical significance at the 1%, 5%, and 10% level respectively.

The first insights on the changes in aid effectiveness between pre- and post-Cold War period correspond to the findings of the aid allocation literature, however, with one additional feature: The existing literature, such as Dollar and Levin (2006: 2041) or Harrigan and Wang (2011: 1290), finds that bilateral donors in general have changed their allocation after the end of the Cold War with an increasing focus on good policies and donor policies, and less oriented towards own goals. Harrigan and Wang (ibid.) conclude that this applies also to the donor countries France, Japan and the UK of G1, but explicitly state that the US are one exception. However, if several bilateral donors are supposed to allocate aid after 1989 significantly "better", one could still expect that the quantitative effectiveness of bilateral and G2 aid increases over the time. When looking at the four coefficients for G2 in each estimation, though, this does not become apparent. The first coefficient for G2 in the left-hand side, representing the impact of G2 aid over 1970-1989 on growth over 1990-2005, is negative but not significant, suggesting that aid payments by G2 donors before the end of the cold war are unrelated with the dependent variable. Looking at the coefficients for the observation period postponed by ten years in both the left- and right-hand side, so that the aid horizon now covers to one half the post-Cold War period, the effect of G2 aid does not appear to change. Proceeding to the aid period 1990-2010, now entirely outside the Cold War era, the coefficient for G2 is smaller but still negative and insignificant.

Quite the contrary applies to G1 aid. The coefficient of the period before the Cold War suggests that aid from G1 donors is positively correlated with growth, but only significant on the 10% level. Looking at the intermediate period, one should start interpreting the coefficient on the right-hand side for reasons of comparability, because both aid and growth horizon are ten years later. The coefficient indicates that G1 aid is stronger correlated with growth, but still weakly significant. When the aid and growth periods overlap (on the left-hand side of the middle row), the observed effect becomes even stronger and gains in significance. This could indicate that when considering a growth period that follows the aid period instead of intersecting it, positive short-run effects of aid are excluded. Now if looking at the post-Cold War period, the coefficient for G1 aid rises again and becomes highly significant.

Both coefficients for BA and MA are insignificant over all observation periods. The estimations suggest that MA does not have a positive impact on growth in neither of the different periods, corresponding to the insight of the cross-sectional investigation of the whole observation period in table 3. The coefficients for BA are negative in the pre-Cold War period and turn positive afterwards. At this point, these observations should not need a detailed interpretation. As discussed in the previous sections, a detailed discussion should take place after achieving further evidence from the more sophisticated panel data approach.

6 Insights from a Dynamic Panel Data Model

Now that first results from a simplified cross-country analysis are achieved, it is time to put these to the test in a more advanced empirical procedure. Because cross-sectional variables are achieved by taking averages over just one period, one of the principal disadvantages of such analyses compared to the use of panel data is that they cannot account for country specific effects. Trumbull and Wall (1994: 867-877) already discuss that this shortcoming can pose a problem in the case of aid studies that usually analyse samples of many recipient countries, which usually involve unobserved specific variables. Looking at the sample and the regression specifications of this this study, for instance, one could imagine that there are various unobserved parameters that have an impact on the explanatory variables. Such determinants could be religion, ethnical composition, the membership of different trade or economic alliances and so on. Applying panel data is an appropriate means of tackling a potential heterogeneity bias. The panel applied in the following consists of five-year averages of each variable, as the original of Rajan and Subramanian (2008: 662). The extended observation period from 2000 to 2014 enables the investigation of three additional periods.

To face the possible heterogeneity bias in an effective way, this chapter applies a GMM estimator, as Hansen and Tarp (2001: 560) suggest for analysing aid effects. This decision is also based on the results of the Hausman specification test for evaluating whether individuals, in this case recipient countries, differ individually from the panel mean over the period or whether deviations are normally distributed (cf. Hausman 1978: 1261-1264). In other word, the test helps to determine whether there are country specific effects among recipients. If this is the case, a fixed effects estimator is the preferred model. The null hypothesis that a random effect model is preferred is rejected across all estimations (p=0.0000), which is why only fixed effects estimation are considered in this chapter (cf. appendix I). Applying a fixed effects estimator also is the appropriate strategy to control for the above-mentioned problem of unobserved heterogeneity between the recipient countries. A further reason for the choice of GMM as the fixed effects estimation strategy is that it is suitable for a panel with a large number of individuals (countries) and a small number of periods (cf. Roodman 2009A: 100), as it is the case in the following analysis.

As indicated in section 2.1, the problem of causality between the right-hand side variables and the dependent variable is one of the most discussed and crucial issues of the aid effectiveness literature, as well as throughout general growth research. This can be explained in the case of the explanatory variables of interest in this study. It is plausible to assume that the effect of aid on growth or the social indicators is not one-sided, as there are several ways in which the dependent variables can also have a reversed impact on aid. If donors solely allocate aid among countries with a very low level of economic development or with poor health conditions, for example, one would always observe a negative relation between these aid flows and the dependent variables without tackling causality. One way to address this issue is to elaborate an instrumentation strategy that to reduces the estimation bias as much as possible (cf.

Boone 1996: 314, Alesina and Dollar 2000: 39 or Dalgaard et al. 2004: 206 amongst others). Because this thesis draws on the specification of Rajan and Subramanian (2008: 651), as one of the most influential studies of the past decade, this type of tackling endogeneity is presumably covered as far as possible.

The application of a GMM panel data estimator, compared to other panel data models, yields a further possibility of treating endogeneity: By adding lagged values of both dependent and explanatory variables as instruments, the issue of endogeneity can directly be addressed (cf. Blundell and Bond 1998: 136). The exact choice of the estimator is the system GMM method of the type suggested by Blundell and Bond (ibid.). As Roodman (2009A: 115) shows, this procedure offers the possibility of including time-invariant regressors by using moment conditions of both first differences and values of residuals. This decision is consistent with the procedure of Headey (2008: 166), Dreher et al. (2008: 300) or Minoiu and Reddy (2010: 36) among others. Estimations are made with the xtabond2 command in Stata that is introduced by Roodman (2009A).

In order to prevent possible bias caused by the GMM estimator as far as possible, this study follows the suggestions of Roodman (2009A, 2009B) and Temple (2010: 4503-4505). First, Roodman (2009A: 116) demonstrates that applicating GMM can, particularly in the case of system GMM, result in a proliferation of partially redundant instruments that can cause considerable bias in estimation results. He therefore suggests restricting the instrument count by either defining lag limits or by collapsing the instruments (cf. ibid.: 108). The main GMM estimations of this study cover both these options. The lag limit of all GMM estimation is reduced to five, in contrast to Rajan and Subramanian (2008: 658), who apply eight lags for the endogenous variables used as instruments.

Therefore, only those results are reported that comply with the rule of thumb that the number of instruments do not outnumber the individuals, i.e. recipient countries in this study. Moreover, the p-values for both the Hansen test for joint validity of the instruments and the Arellano-Bond test for autocorrelation are added to the results, to demonstrate that instruments are not overused. A short interpretation of these values follows in the subsequent section when reporting the first results. The estimations additionally include a set of time dummies to support the assumption that there is no correlation across individuals in the idiosyncratic error, as Roodman (2009A: 102) recommends

All results in this chapter only report the coefficients of the explanatory of interest, i.e. MA, BA, G1 aid and G2 aid. Appendices E and F show the full result tables. In order to address the above-mentioned issue of instrument proliferation, the results also include the number of instruments, as well as the p-values for the Hansen and Arellano-Bond tests. Equal to the previous chapter, the analysis of growth effects is first carried out, followed by the social indicators estimations. A third section tests for robustness of the panel data evidence.

6.1 Reinvestigating the effect on growth

The application of panel data involves further improvements for reaching the scientific goals of this thesis. First, it helps to determine more precisely whether aid effectiveness changes during the post-Cold War period. The subsequent main estimations in section 6.1 analyse both the whole observation period and, in addition, all periods after the year 1989. The aim this is to provide an explicit comparison of the temporal changes in aid coefficients. Moreover, it enables to address the issue of delayed aid effects. One can now take into account the assumption that aid effects arrive after a considerable delay by lagging the variables. It is important to note, once again, that total undivided aid numbers of the individual donors shall be considered. A different approach would be, as Clemens et al. (2012: 599) for instance do, to remove all aid flows that are not supposed to affect aid within a certain period from the estimations. As discussed before, however, this involves the danger of omitting aid flows that potentially hamper growth, and which certain donors possibly more often disburse than others. Therefore, the procedure of the following analyses rather is to differentiate between four different lag lengths for the total aid flows of each donor, representing time intervals of 5, 10 and 15 years, respectively.

All the following estimation results are based on the same regression equation system that is set up in chapter 5 with the purpose of separating MA and BA, as well as the two donor groups, respectively. One new feature is that the error term is decomposed into the unobserved time invariant country specific effects μ_i, as depicted in the previous section, and random noise υ_i such that $\varepsilon_i = \mu_i + \upsilon_i$ (cf. Blundell and Bond: 1998: 117). Additionally, lagged values of the variables are added. Like in the original approach of Rajan and Subramanian (2008: 659), all explanatory variables are treated as endogenous, except geography and the time dummies. Compared to the cross-sectional analysis, one additional change is made regarding the control variables. The original policy variable, initially introduced by Wacziarg and Welch (2008), only covers the period until 1999. In order to maintain an indicator for openness that, however, covers the whole period until 2014, the original index is replaced by the WDI measure for openness that is proxied by the ratio of trade to GDP (cf. appendix B1). Table 7 presents the estimation results for the aid-growth part that includes a differentiation between pre- and post-Cold War period. For both periods, each comprising the three different estimations, all four time lags are considered.

When comparing the GMM results of the whole period, in the upper half of table 7, with

Table 7: *Aid and growth: GMM panel data evidence*

	(1)	(2)	(3)	(4)	(5)	(6)	(7)	(8)	(9)
Whole Period									
Lag length		5 years			10 years			15 years	
G1 aid	48.56*			47.36***			24.05		
	(27.24)			(17.52)			(24.13)		
G2 aid		4.095			7.575			-17.43	
		(24.19)			(18.25)			(19.79)	
BA			0.728			7.605			-6.770
			(11.31)			(10.49)			(7.795)
MA			42.76*			7.904			16.26
			(23.74)			(18.22)			(19.57)
Observations	526	526	526	526	526	526	526	526	526
Post-Cold War period									
	(1)	(2)	(3)	(4)	(5)	(6)	(7)	(8)	(9)
Lag length		5 years			10 years			15 years	
G1 aid	54.32**			37.81***			20.96		
	(23.74)			(13.40)			(19.85)		
G2 aid		-11.84			8.153			-26.62	
		(20.04)			(18.05)			(20.07)	
BA			-0.850			9.502			7.675
			(14.40)			(9.720)			(11.75)
MA			9.795			3.753			-12.24
			(25.54)			(26.02)			(19.76)
Observations	350	350	350	350	350	350	350	350	350

Sources: Author's calculations.
Notes: The dependent variables is the average annual growth rate of GDP per capita. Only coefficients of the explanatory variables of interest are reported, appendix E shows the full estimations. Robust standard errors in parentheses. For descriptions of the variables and their sources, see B1. ***, ** and * denote statistical significance at the 1%, 5%, and 10% level respectively.

the estimations in table 3, it becomes evident that most of the re-estimated coefficients coincide with the first cross-sectional indications. A first observation that is confirmed is the ineffectiveness of both multilateral and total bilateral aid. Among all three time lags; shown in columns 3, 6 and 9, estimated parameters for BA and MA are insignificant with only one exception. The weakly significant coefficient for five-year lagged MA shall not be further addressed, as it does not prove to be robust. This finding is in line with a widely-held opinion of the aid-growth literature - cf. Boone 1996: 312, Easterly et al. 2004: 775, Roodman 2007: 270-271 or Doucouliagos and Paldam 2009: 453, to name just a few of the most influential studies. Above all, it is in line with the original results of Rajan and Subramanian (2008: 658). Since one of the objectives was not to change the original results by making too many modifications of the instrumentation strategy, as mentioned in section 5.1, this is an important feature and a big difference to Arndt el al. (2010: 15-17), who find a positive and significant impact of aid on growth after altering the original specifications of Rajan and Subramanian (2008). A closer look at the results for G1 and G2 could provide an explanation why aid research so often fails to find a significant effect of total aid numbers.

To begin with the effect of G1 aid, the coefficients of the GMM analysis also prove to correspond with the first insights of the cross-sectional part. Their values closely coincide with the initial one in table 3 (49,39). Considering the whole observation period, however, the coefficient for five-year lagged G1 aid (column 1) is only weakly significant. When looking at the 15-year lag (column 9), it is not even significant at all. On the other hand, the coefficient for G1 aid with a lag of ten years (column 4) proves to be highly significant and indicates that an increase in G1 aid to GDP of one percentage point is correlated with a higher GDP growth per capita of about 0.6 percentage points after a period of ten years. The results for G2 aid, however, are not precisely confirmed. Neither of the coefficients for lagged G2 aid shows to be significant, in contrast to the initial pointer that G2 aid has a negative and significant impact on growth. After having reinvestigated the more drastic insight of the cross-sectional part, one should now rather interpret that the results suggest G2 aid to be unrelated with growth.

These observations confirm the insights of the aid allocation literature. They do also match the estimation results of Minoiu and Reddy (2010: 36), whose coefficients for G1 aid are highly positive and partially significant. One major difference, however, applies to the lag of aid effects. Minoiu and Reddy (ibid.) determine a highly significant coefficient the for five-year lagged G1 aid, and moderately significant coefficients for the lags of 15 and 25 years. Moreover, after including Belgium, France, Ireland, Switzerland, and the United Kingdom; as countries that are classically regarded as donors with a higher focus on own interest; Minoiu and Reddy (ibid.) find that the impact of aid is lower in extent and only moderately significant after a lag of five years, and loses significance with a value close to zero considering the 15- and 25-year lags. When looking at generous donors (G1) and more self-interested donors (G2) separately, this observation effectively corresponds to the findings of this study.

A core question that now arises is why G1 aid appears to be this highly correlated with growth of recipient countries, whereas G2 aid does not show to have any effect at all. Plausible explanations for the high extent of the coefficients for G1 aid are provided by the aid allocation literature. As section 2.3.1 presents in detail, several studies find that aid of Scandinavian countries, and a few other donors such as the Netherlands or Iceland, allocate aid mainly to countries with high humanitarian and development needs, as well as to those countries that prove to have good policies or to meet basic rights (cf. Alesina and Dollar 2000: 47, Dreher et al. 2010: 167, Berthélemy 2006A: 191 or Gates and Hoeffler 2004). One straightforward interpretation is that the estimations of this thesis could simply approve the findings of the aid allocation literature on a quantitative level. Accordingly, the negative and not significant coefficients of G2 aid could likewise be quantifications for the insights of Alesina and Dollar (2000: 43-44), Kilby and Dreher (2010: 340) or Tierney et al. (2011: 1899-1900) that G2 countries allocate their aid with a considerably strong focus on strategic interests. These differences in aid allocation are certainly a main reference point for interpreting the clearly diverging results.

A less critical argumentation is the following: As we can see in table 2, G1 donors allocate their aid mainly to smaller countries in terms of economy and population number, many of which located in SSA; such as Zambia, Mozambique, Tanzania,

Uganda or Ethiopia. It is conceivable that aid flows to countries with a low initial level of economic development can result in a higher marginal growth compared to such flows to larger countries with an already intermediate level of economy. Accordingly, the high G2 aid flows to China, Egypt or Indonesia for instance, could result in a lower impact on growth for the same reasons. Despite their higher level of GDP per capita, these countries still, without any doubt, have large needs for development assistance in many areas.

Nevertheless, an equal amount of aid per GDP should result in a lower level of GDP per capita growth according to basic growth theories. Because the aid allocation literature in general uses average values of development indicators, such as per capita growth, for the estimation of recipient needs (cf. Alesina and Dollar 2000: 57 or Levin and Dollar 2006: 2042), while economically more advanced recipient countries often have high inequality levels and, thus, can have large shares of the population living in poverty, the recipient needs argument does not necessarily have to be an essential cause for the divergence results between G1 and G2 aid. However, the orientation towards recipient needs is not the only parameter that can be derived from the aid allocation literature. The stronger focus on own strategic interest or the disregarding of good policy environments in recipient countries by G2 donors, as stated by Berthélemy (2006A: 183), Kilby and Dreher (2010: 340) or Harrigan and Wang (2011: 1284) among others, cannot be explained with this line of argument.

The strikingly different results for G1 and G2 aid effectiveness once again prompt to reflect the ineffectiveness of total bilateral aid numbers. It is evident that a separation of similar donors into groups is a right strategy to elaborate on the question why aid so often proves to be ineffective. Yet, it is desirable to know more about the results for each single donor, to obtain a more precise picture of which types of aid appear to be effective and which not. Harrigan and Wang (2011: 1290), for instance, find that the UK, Japan and France show an increasing focus on good policy environments over the latest decades, whereas the respective explanatory variable for US aid does not prove to increase. Nevertheless, a closer look on the individual donors' aid effectiveness would require further disaggregation and, for the resulting smaller aid numbers, possibly imply more empirical challenges.

At this point, the timing of aid effects needs to be discussed once more. As Clemens et al. (2012: 594) state, the question of which time period to consider for analysing lagged aid effects remains disputed. The approach of this section, i.e. differentiating between three different lag length, provides insight into this issue. This procedure is similar to the one of Minoiu and Reddy (2010: 36), who, however, consider time lags of 5, 15, and 25 years. The results of this study indicate that G1 aid effectiveness increases with higher time lags. As the coefficient for the 15-year lag is not significant anymore, however, one could argue that most of the aid effects arrive within a period of five to ten years after aid has been disbursed. This finding contrasts with the results of Minoiu and Reddy (ibid.), who still find a highly positive and moderately significant impact of G1 aid on growth after a lag of 25 years. However, it is in line with the consideration of Clemens et al. (2012: 594), who argue that several types of aid show a relatively early impact.

Now, when looking at the lower half of table 7, a further supposition of the cross-sectional chapter turns out to point in the right direction. The coefficient for five-year lagged G1 aid is considerably higher when looking at the post-Cold War period. The respective correlation after the ten-year lag is still shows to be highly significant, however, also noticeably lower. One should still bear mind that the post-Cold War period only covers 25 years. As lagging the variables for ten years reduces the observable effect to 15 years, the lower correlation between G1 aid and growth must not necessarily point towards lower effectiveness.

The coefficients for MA and BA remain insignificant over all time lags. The same applies to G2 aid, which even shows to negative, but still not significant coefficients. These results suggest that countries of G1 have slightly improved their aid practices, whereas aid effectiveness of G2 donors is unchanged. This is in line with the findings of Berthélemy (2006A: 192), who argues that the egoistic aid allocation of major bilateral donors, among them four of the G2 countries, do not change after the end of the Cold War. One reason why G1 aid appears to be (moderately) more effective after 1989 could be a stronger orientation towards recipient needs. It is also conceivable that aid donors generally have learned more about good aid practices over the considered time frame. However, the change in aid allocation of individual G1 donors should be analysed into more detail to provide an accurate statement on this.

Even if the results in table 7 do not point towards a significant negative effect of G2 aid, the fact that all G2 coefficients among both cross-sectional and GMM estimations partially have a negative sign requires further explanation, as Temple (2010: 4448) suggests that all indications for aid to be potentially harmful should be discussed with care. Again, it needs to be noted that this thesis does not understand the estimation results as evidence for a negative effect of G2 aid, but rather as an absence of evidence for a positive effect or, at most, a weak tendency towards a negative effect. Nevertheless, as there are plausible explanations why aid can have a negative effect on growth within the literature, it appears reasonable to take a glance at the argumentation of negative aid effects. Against the background that aid accounts for a large share of the government budget of many recipient countries[12], Djankov et al. (2008: 179) show that higher aid

---

[12]Djankov et al. (2008: 169-170) state that aid accounted for two thirds of the government budget of Burkina Faso during the period 1985-1989, for 60% in Mauretania in 1980-1984 and for over one third in several other SSA countries.

receipts are correlated with a weakening of policy institution and compare this finding to the negative effects caused by the abundance of a natural resource such as oil. In the same vein, Rajan and Subramanian (2007: 324) demonstrate that aid has a significantly negative impact on the domestic manufacturing sector in recipient countries. In addition to the negative effects of high amounts of aid, Kimura et al. (2012: 7-8) find that if many donors operate in one recipient country, each of them with its own aid agencies and projects, aid decreases bureaucratic quality and can be harmful for growth.

If one bears in mind that G2 aid flows account for a large share of total aid numbers, the insight that too much aid can be harmful corresponds to the findings. It is, for instance, conceivable that only a certain share of G2 aid, or only flows to certain recipients, effect growth negatively, whereas other types of aid could show a similar effect to G1 aid. The latter finding of Kimura et al (ibid.) could also have some explanatory power for the findings of G2 aid effectivity. As appendix C3 shows, several countries receive aid flows from various G2 donors. In the case that the assistance is not coordinated effectively between the different donors, and that each aid agency requires its own bureaucratic processes, one could imagine that aid might involve increased efforts or even risks for the recipient countries.

At this point, the discussion shall return to the empirical issues mentioned in the introductory part of this chapter. The full estimation results, shown in appendices E and F, prove that the choice of instrumentation complies with the suggestions from the previous literature. First, the instrument count is below the number of recipient countries among all the estimations, meaning that the rule of thumb according to Roodman (2009A: 99) is covered. Second, the reported p-values of the Hansen test for overidentifying restrictions are reasonably low. This test is used for verifying the appropriate use of the GMM-style instruments of lagged explanatory variables (cf. Roodman 2009B: 143). Roodman (ibid.: 151) states that perfect Hansen p-values of 1.000 are a warning signal for instrument proliferation. On the other hand, Hansen p-values below 0.05 also indicate that chosen instruments potentially imply biased results (cf. ibid: 153). As appendices E and F show, neither of these two cases is present among the GMM estimations of this study. Third, all p-values for the Arellano-Bond test, in the appendices reported as AR(2) are higher than 0.05. This additional test for autocorrelation verifies the use of lagged instrument variables. Rejecting the null hypothesis of this test, i.e. $p < 0.05$, would indicate that the application of lagged explanatory variables in the instrumentation is inappropriate (cf. Roodman 2009A: 119).

6.2 Reinvestigating the effect on social indicators

The main reassessment of the effects on social indicators is also based on GMM dynamic panel data methodology. As for the aid-growth specification, the Hausman test for both the infant mortality and primary completion regression indicates that a fixed data approach is preferable (cf. appendices I2 and I3). Masud and Yontcheva (2005: 13) also analyse the effect on infant mortality using a fixed effects estimator. However, for analysing the correlation between aid and illiteracy, Masud und Yontcheva (2005: 14) apply a random effects model after finding endogeneity of several regressors. The GMM approach, however, particularly deals with the problem of endogenous variables and still has the advantage of considering fixed effects. Since the mutual relations between the social indicators and its regressors, as well as the issue of country specific characteristic among the sample of aid recipients are not less severe than in the aid-growth analysis, an investigation based on a GMM estimator is the preferable approach. As we well see, moreover, the observation period of the following analysis is even shorter than in the previous section. Because this is a further feature that can be dealt with by applying a GMM approach, and for the reasons of comparability, the investigation the impact on primary completion also apply this method.

A separate treatment of pre-and post-Cold War periods as in the previous section cannot be applied to the panel data analyses of neither of the social indicator regressions, for reasons of data availability. Several of the explanatory variables, especially the ones for both types of public expenditures and the poverty headcount, as well as data for the two dependent variables are not available until the late 1980s or early 1990s. Recording of health expenditures data, for instance, only begins in 1995. For this reason, estimation results for both primary completion and infant mortality are presented for only one period, beginning with 1990. The poor data availability for indicators in the areas of health and education is also why female literacy, as a control variable for the infant mortality regression, is dropped in the main panel data approach.

The results are, again, presented for three different time lags, covering the emergence of aid effects up to a period of 15 years. Table 8 lists the estimation results for both infant mortality, in the upper half, and primary completion, in the lower half.

Equal to the previous section, the results of the social indicator regressions largely coincide with the cross-sectional insights. The four different aid variables in the infant mortality estimations differ among the donors in extent and show the right expected signs to continue the interpretation of the previous section, but neither of the coefficients shows significance. Regarding primary completion, only one the result for ten-year lagged BA proves to be moderately significant. This finding, however, is not robust changes of any kind, as the robustness test shows. The results, therefore, again suggest

Table 8: *Aid and social indicators: GMM panel data evidence*

	(1)	(2)	(3)	(4)	(5)	(6)	(7)	(8)	(9)
	Dependent variable: Infant Mortality								
Lag length	5 years			10 years			15 years		
G1 aid	0.445			-1.038			0.361		
	-5.71			(3.250)			(2.071)		
G2 aid		-0.295			-0.0689			-0.771	
		(2.735)			(1.276)			(2.507)	
BA			0.589			0.0805			-0.528
			(1.378)			(1.200)			(0.419)
MA			-2.937			-0.176			-1.323
			(2.774)			(1.499)			(1.992)
Ovservations	242	242	242	242	242	242	242	242	242

	(1)	(2)	(3)	(4)	(5)	(6)	(7)	(8)	(9)
	Dependent variable: Primary Completion								
Lag length	5 years			10 years			15 years		
G1 aid	-4.949			2.006			0.717		
	(5.147)			(3.387)			(4.320)		
G2 aid		-1.619			-2.679			-0.543	
		(2.155)			(3.319)			(1.871)	
BA			-2.156			-2.985**			-1.675
			(1.892)			(1.374)			(1.944)
MA			-2.991			0.229			4.009
			(2.942)			(2.267)			(3.670)
Ovservations	228	228	228	228	228	228	228	228	228

Sources: Author's calculations.
Notes: The dependent variables are the average annual rate of infant mortality in the upper half, and the average annual rate of primary completion in the lower part. The observation period is 1990-2014 respectively. Only coefficients of the explanatory variables of interest are reported, appendix F shows the full estimations. Robust standard errors in parentheses. For descriptions of the variables and their sources, see appendix B1.
***, ** and * denote statistical significance at the 1%, 5%, and 10% level respectively.

that aid flows from all donors are uncorrelated with improvements in social welfare. This is a striking result that requires a deeper discussion.

To begin with the argumentation of Masud and Yontcheva (2005: 20) as the work that provides the original specifications for this section. After finding a significant positive impact of NGO aid on infant mortality and no effect of BA on neither of the social variables, Masud and Yontcheva (ibid.) interpret their results based on the stronger orientation of NGOs aid towards the needs among the poor population in recipient countries. Thus, one could argue that one reason why G1 does not appear to positively affect social indicators, relates to differences in the way bilateral donors implement aid at the recipient level, compared to the aid practice of NGOs, for instance. This assumption is confirmed by Dreher et al. (2010: 153), who compare the aid allocation of Swedish bilateral and NGO aid and find that a large share of NGO aid is targeted to the sectors health, education and human rights and, consequently, intended to benefit the poor more directly than bilateral aid with a stronger focus on economic areas. After analysing the aid allocation of both NGOs and BA in more detail with respect to several measures for recipient needs, Dreher et al. (2010: 163) conclude that NGOs respond more quickly to emergency needs of recipient countries due to their closeness to the affected population. The fact that NGOs are closer to the poor and often have their own health or education projects, whereas bilateral aid rather aims at improving the domestic economy, could be a reason why aid variables of this study do not appear to be positively correlated with the social indicators.

This argument, however, appears to have one loophole: Boone (1996: 293) claims that infant mortality can be used as a key indicator for measuring the economic improvements of the poor population. Moreover, Bloom et al. (2004, 10) show that better health conditions have a significant positive impact on higher economic growth. One could, therefore, interpret the missing relation between G1 aid and the social measures, considering that G1 does affect growth positively, as evidence for a similar conclusion to that of Boone (1996: 322). After finding no positive effect of aid on growth but a significant positive impact on government consumption, Boone (ibid.) concludes that aid would only appear to support wealthy political regimes. Since G1 shows a positive effect on growth in this study, however, this kind of interpretation would be too drastic. One could rather argue, for instance, that G1 aid manages to effectively strengthen the domestic industry or infrastructure of recipient countries and, while doing so, to improve the economic situation of highly skilled workers. The poor or rural population, according to this argumentation, might not benefit from G1 aid.

The insight that bilateral aid fails to improve the living conditions of the poor is in line with previous findings of the literature. Alvi and Senbeta (2012: 968), for instance, work out that BA has no effect on neither poverty rate nor poverty gap. However, they also find that MA has a significant negative impact on both measures, suggesting that it is effective in alleviating poverty among recipient countries and, thus, directly benefits the poor. As we can see in table 8, this insight is not supported by the results of this study. All MA coefficients for both social indicators are insignificant and close to zero.

Besides an economic interpretation, the lack of evidence may also have empirical reasons. Gomanee et al. (2005B: 301) and Dreher et al. (2008: 294) argue that aid is often targeted at increasing pro-poor government expenditures. Since health and education expenditures are included in the respective estimation equations of this section, the possibility that aid has a positive impact on these is omitted. The robustness check, however, covers this issue by leaving out the control variables for public expenditures. As the next section shows, this does still not increase the impact of aid. Another issue of an empirical nature is the low availability of data in the social areas of developing countries, as mentioned above. Firstly, this resulted in a restriction to the observation period. Secondly, despite considering only the period 1990-2014 for the two social indicators, data are still less available than for the post-Cold War investigation of the growth effects. As Appendices E and F show, observations in the social-indicator data are significantly lower in number than in the aid-growth analysis. It is conceivable that this lack of data impairs the quality of estimation results. A further objective of the robustness check, therefore, is to systematically add observations to the estimations by gradually leaving out control variables.

6.3 Robustness tests

Up to this point, the following main results are consistent throughout both cross-sectional and dynamic panel data analyses: First, total bilateral as well as multilateral aid do not show a significant effect neither on growth nor on one of the social indicators. Second, concerning the effect on growth, there appears to be a striking difference between G1 and G2 aid. Whereas the findings suggest that G2 and growth are uncorrelated, coefficients for G1 aid are highly positive and significant among all estimations. Third, this observation, however, cannot be made when looking at the impact on infant mortality or primary completion. Because these findings are confirmed in two approaches that are both frequently applied in the aid effectiveness literature, one can argue that they are already robust to a certain degree. To increase robustness of the panel data results, this section follows two different approaches.

The first series of robustness tests re-evaluates the GMM results with the help of different panel data estimators. Several studies, particularly in recent years, point out that GMM estimators are not a panacea in the field of aid effectiveness research. As discussed in section 2.1, a key issue of aid effectiveness research is the choice of instrumentation strategy. Clemens et al. (2012: 595-957) examine the approaches of influential aid effectiveness studies and conclude that there are no reliable instruments for aid. They argue, moreover, that existing GMM estimators do no offer the possibility to explicitly test for weak instruments. A further issue, as mentioned in the introductory part of this chapter, concerns the excessive use of instrument additionally created by GMM estimators. Roodman (2009A: 98-99), as well as Temple (2010: 4503) state that too many instruments can also cause considerable bias in the results.

Addressing these methodical problems, Clemens et al. (2012: 597) argue that applying a GMM approach does not necessarily reduce the bias of results. Therefore, they limit their estimations to the reassessment of existing OLS regressions of Boone (1996), Burnside and Dollar (2000) and Rajan and Subramanian (2008) without instrumenting for aid. By allowing for lagged aid effects, extending the observation period and restricting aid to those flows that are supposed to have an effect in the short run, Clemens et al. (2012: 603-608) find a moderately positive effect of aid on growth among all three specifications. Following the approach of Clemens et al. (ibid.), a first procedure for testing the panel data results for robustness is a simple OLS estimator. Further estimations that avoid the above-mentioned problems are based on an additional fixed effects estimator, equal to the approach of Boone (1996: 305) or Masud and Yontcheva (2005:13). The results of this first series of robustness test are shown in table 9 for the effect in growth, with a differentiation between pre- and post-Cold War period similar to table 7, and in table 10 for the effects on infant mortality and primary completion, referring to table 8. For each period two FE estimation results are reported:

The former examines the effect of the current aid flows as explanatory variable of interest, and the latter reassesses the influence of aid lagged over two periods, i.e. ten years. The objective behind this differentiation is to retest the assumption that aid effects arrive after a certain period.

Table 9: *Robustness of panel data estimations - the effect on growth*

	Whole Period								
Estimator	(1) OLS	(2)	(3)	(4) FE	(5)	(6)	(7) FE	(8)	(9)
G1 aid	50.03***			21.03			32.21**		
	(17.93)			(16.91)			-12.8		
G2 aid		-12.73*			-10.05			-1.506	
		(7.288)			(8.444)			-6.932	
BA			-1.349			-2.732			-0.968
			(5.616)			(5.813)			-5.11
MA			-1.014			4.382			8.307
			(8.148)			(9.885)			-8.076
Lag length	-	-	-	-	-	-		10 years	
Observations	570	570	570	570	570	570	624	624	624

	Post-Cold War period								
Estimator	(1) OLS	(2)	(3)	(4) FE	(5)	(6)	(7) FE	(8)	(9)
G1 aid	61.17***			44.43**			31.14**		
	(22.58)			(22.28)			-15.12		
G2 aid		-11.18			1.088			-4.288	
		(10.89)			(10.99)			-9.383	
BA			-2.617			-0.296			4.713
			(6.806)			(6.670)			-6.125
MA			-4.199			3.446			5.47
			(8.896)			(12.10)			-9.79
Lag length	-	-	-	-	-	-		10 years	
Observations	392	392	392	392	392	392	421	421	421

Sources: Author's calculations.
Notes: Columns 1-3 report OLS-, columns 4-9 fixed effects (FE) estimation results. The dependent variable is the average annual GDP growth rate per capita. Only coefficients of the explanatory variables of interest are reported, appendices G1 and G2 show the full estimations. Robust standard errors in parentheses. For descriptions of the variables and their sources, see appendix B1. ***, ** and * denote statistical significance at the 1%, 5%, and 10% level respectively.

A first look at table 9 reveals that the main results largely coincide with both cross-sectional and GMM estimations. The non-existing effects of BA, MA, and G2, as well as the positive and significant effect of G2 aid are confirmed. The only coefficient of G1 aid that does not show to be significantly positive is the one of the FE estimation with the non-lagged level of aid for the whole observation period in in column 4. As the coefficient of two-period lagged G1 aid in column 7 is (moderately) significant, however, this can be considered as further indication that the effects of aid occur with a considerably high time lag. Among all additional estimations, moreover, G1 aid shows to have a considerably higher effect during the post-Cold War period.

Appendices H1 and H2 show additional estimations based on difference GMM method. This choice rests upon the above-mentioned problem of instrument proliferation. As Roodman (2009A: 148) states, system GMM generally produces more instruments and, thus, is more sensitive to this issue. Applying the difference GMM estimator, again applying both options of limiting the lags and collapsing the instruments, leads to the weakest result of G1 aid. As appendix H shows, however, both coefficients for ten-year lagged aid are highly positive and significant. Therefore, these estimations still strongly indicate that aid effectiveness differs between G1 and G2.

A further line of estimations, shown in table 10, test for the robustness of the infant mortality and primary completion results. As explained in the previous section, data for the social indicator regressions is very limited. For this reason, the objective now is to systematically increase the number of observations by applying changes to the specification. Masud and Yontcheva (2005,13-14) already report their main results with three different variations of the specification for each of the indicators. In addition to the full set of control variables, they leave out distinct variables for which data is particularly scarce. In order to provide comparability with the original results, the following robustness estimations are based on the original specification changes. This includes OLS and FE estimators, similar to the previous investigation of the growth effect. The latter one is also applied in the original by Masud and Yontcheva (2005: 13) for one of the infant mortality estimations. In addition to the results in table 10, a second table in appendices H3 and H4 shows the results for specification changes based on the previously applied GMM estimator, to thoroughly check their sensitivity to increases in observations.

Table 10: *Robustness of panel data estimations - the effect on social indicators*

	Dependent variable: Infant Mortality								
Estimator	(1) OLS	(2)	(3)	(4) FE	(5)	(6)	(7) FE	(8)	(9)
G1 aid	-0.629			2.990			-0.690		
	(4.607)			(3.195)			(1.540)		
G2 aid		-0.268			2.111**			1.159	
		(2.077)			(0.998)			(0.770)	
BA			-1.982			1.147*			0.474
			(1.553)			(0.668)			(0.467)
MA			1.043			0.409			-0.143
			(1.920)			(0.741)			(0.790)
Variables dropped	-	-	-	-	-	-		health expenditures	
Observations	243	243	243	243	243	243	336	336	336

	Dependent variable: Primary Completion								
Estimator	(1) OLS	(2)	(3)	(4) FE	(5)	(6)	(7) FE	(8)	(9)
G1 aid	3.731*			0.353			0.965		
	(2.036)			(1.678)			(1.674)		
G2 aid		-3.178**			-3.017***			-2.933***	
		(1.604)			(0.896)			(0.829)	
BA			-1.065			-1.837***			-1.210**
			(0.772)			(0.504)			(0.546)
MA			-1.199			0.283			0.0233
			(1.069)			(0.978)			(0.812)
Variables dropped	-	-	-	-	-	-		poverty, institutional quality	
Observations	256	256	256	256	256	256	483	483	483

Sources: Author's calculations.
Notes: Columns 1-3 report OLS-, columns 4-9 fixed effects (FE) estimation results. The dependent variables are the average annual rate of infant mortality in the upper half, and the average annual rate of primary completion in the lower part. The observation period is 1990-2014 respectively. Only coefficients of the explanatory variables of interest are reported, appendices G3 and G4 show the full estimations. Robust standard errors in parentheses. For descriptions of the variables and their sources, see appendix B1. ***, ** and * denote statistical significance at the 1%, 5%, and 10% level respectively.

The insights of the social indicator estimations also prove to be robust, with one exception: Whereas MA and G1 aid again do not show to affect neither of the dependent variables, neglecting the weak significance of G1 aid in the OLS estimations of the primary completion effect in column 1, BA and especially G2 aid now show several significant coefficients. This applies especially to the estimations of the effect on primary completion that are shown in the lower part of table 10. As the signs of these coefficients indicate a potentially harmful effect of the two aid variables in both infant mortality and primary completion regressions, and because several results of the additional GMM-based robustness test in appendices H3-H4 point in the same direction, it is again worth taking a closer look at this observation.

First, it could be possible that bilateral aid has in fact a harmful influence on social indicators, let it be primary completion for the following interpretation. As discussed in section 5.1, the literature already provides sound reasons why high amounts of aid can have an adverse impact on growth in recipient countries. Hence, one could also argue that the negative coefficients of G2 aid in the primary completion estimations coincide with the findings of Djankov et al. (2008: 179) and Kimura et al. (2012: 7-8), i.e. high aid flows from multiple donors can cause similar problems to the abundance of a natural resource by weakening local institutions and slowing down bureaucratic processes. In the case of primary completion, this could imply a negative effect on the quality of domestic education policies for instance.

The finding that G2 and BA show significantly negative coefficients, on the other hand, is not consistent with the insights of the main GMM analysis in table 8. They are, consequently, not robust to changes in the specification or to different estimators. The chosen system GMM method is, however, the preferred estimator for good reasons. One of the main reasons for this choice, as depicted in chapter 6, is that it deals with the endogeneity problem by adding lagged values of the variables, whereas FE estimation results are possibly characterised by a certain level of bias. The results of the GMM-based estimations in appendix H3 and H4, furthermore, potentially leave out important control variables. As we can see in columns 5,6 and 9 of appendix H4, the coefficients for G2 aid and BA only become significantly negative after dropping initial income and institutional quality as two highly meaningful variables for explaining changes in primary completion. For these reasons, it is adequate to conclude that there is still not enough evidence for a clear negative effect of the two aid variables.

7 Policy Implications

Referring back to the title of this thesis, the empirical results that have been achieved in this thesis allow to draw a rather negative conclusion regarding the role of aid in reaching global development goals. As a large body of the aid effectiveness literature already indicates, the findings of this study support the conclusion that there is a need for urgent changes of common aid practices if international donors want to contribute to achieving commonly defined development goals. This becomes apparent first when looking at the aid allocation of major donors (section 4.2) and is confirmed by quantitative analyses of the aid effects.

With the objective of identifying more satisfying aid practices, several previous studies find that aid from multilateral donors shows significantly better effects on development indicators, such as Alvi and Senbeta (2012: 965) in the case of poverty alleviation or Headey (2008: 170) regarding the effect on growth. Throughout all the results of this thesis; and this includes three different indicators, four different estimation methods, different time horizons and lags, as well as changes in the specifications; this result cannot be confirmed. Although this study does not explicitly analyse the way in which multilateral donors allocate aid, the results suggest that MA and BA do not significantly differ regarding the main motives of aid allocation. This observation is in line with the results of Rajan and Subramanian (2008: 656), and may reflect the conclusion of Berthélemy (2006B: 99) that multilateral aid allocation is significantly influenced by the commercial interest of individual shareholders, such as the US. Therefore, the logical implication of the results is, in contrast to the advice of previous investigations, that it is implausible to direct larger aid shares through multilateral agencies.

The disaggregation of bilateral aid flows, as the main research focus of this thesis, allows to draw several meaningful conclusions. An argument that is often put forward is that the aid allocation of major bilateral donors is largely determined by economic interests and power-political motives. Provided that this is the main cause behind the finding that G1 aid shows a highly positive and significant effect on growth across all estimations, whereas G2 aid appears to be generally non-effective and even shows a slightly negative impact in some of the results, it would be pointless to draw policy lessons for bilateral aid agencies. Notwithstanding, several other parties could profit from these insights. Creating a stronger awareness about aid that is ineffective or potentially harmful may directly benefit the recipient countries, as they ultimately had the discretion to reject certain kinds of aid. Another possibility for this insight to be transferred into practice is that the international donor community sets common rules to prevent the misuse or overuse of aid. Analogous laws might also be established by international legislation.

If, however, other causes than economic or political motives are substantially responsible for the ineffectiveness of G2 aid, or MA and BA in general, one can directly draw implications for the respective aid agencies. Insights of the aid allocation literature provide good explanations for the finding that G1 aid is the only aid variable of this study that shows a positive effect on growth. A first implication can be derived from the finding that several smaller bilateral donors, among them Scandinavian countries, Canada, Iceland or the Netherlands; show to allocate their aid mainly to small countries that are considered as LDCs (cf. Alesina and Dollar 2000: 50 or Berthélemy 2006A: 190-191). As appendix C2 shows, this feature is confirmed for the allocation of all G1 donors. Quite the contrary applies to G2 donors, see appendix C3, which seem to favour economically more advanced recipient countries.

Now one could imagine that this difference is not merely based on different motives of the donors. The size of economy of the preferred recipient countries might, for instance, also be a consequence of the greatly varying aid budgets of G1 and G2 donors. It is easy to picture that small countries with a rather limited aid budget simply chose small recipient countries, as their funds might just not be enough to cover the costs of aid programmes in larger recipient countries, whereas the major bilateral donors could have sufficiently high budgets to supply the needs of countries such as India, Indonesia or Egypt. There are also several plausible reasons why aid does not show to positively affect growth of economically more advanced countries. The finding of Rajan and Subramanian (2007: 324) that aid has an adverse effect on the size of the domestic industry in recipient countries could, for instance, indicates that it might not be appropriate to intervene the economy of already more developed countries with large amounts of aid. Nevertheless, despite the possible existence of less critical causes behind different aid allocations, a logical conclusion from these observations is that redirecting aid to countries with a weaker economic development should achieve a higher total impact on GDP growth across the recipient countries.

When looking once again at the aid distribution of individual G2 donors in Appendix C3, another insight of the previous may explain why G2 aid does not show to be positively related with growth. Many countries, such as Bangladesh, Egypt, India, Israel or Pakistan, receive high amounts of assistance from several G2 donors. If one bears in mind that each of the donors has its own aid agency that demands its own bureaucratic procedures, it would seem obvious that recipients face high extra efforts when they engage with multiple donors at the same time – not to forget that there are more bilateral donors than G1 and G2 countries and a high number of multilateral agencies as well. As discussed in the previous section, this presumption is in line with the finding of Kimura et al. (2012: 7-8) and Djankov et al. (2008: 179) that high aid flows by various donors can hamper institutional quality and, thus, have a negative effect on growth.

One straightforward answer to this problem could be that donors must precisely coordinate all their aid activities for each of the recipient. This could be implemented, just to give one example, by organisations that are formed across the donors with the aim of not only directing aid flows, but also determining which amount and type of aid would be best for each recipient. This would also be an effective way to eliminate individual donor interests.

A final point concerns the finding that none of the investigated donors shows to have a positive impact on either of the two chosen social areas, regardless of the estimation method, observation period or the number of lags. As mentioned before, it is possible that aid increases health or education expenditures and eventually via this channel achieves a positive outcome (cf. Gomanee et al. 2005B: 301). This study does not explicitly test this possible causation for the different aid variables of interest. Masud and Yontcheva (2005: 17-19), however, already find that total BA does neither increase health nor education expenditures. Moreover, omitting the expenditures variables from the regressions, as appendices H1 and H2 show, does not increase the effect of the aid variables. It is therefore very likely that the aid variables of this study do not significantly affect governments expenditures in the two social areas either. If that is the case, one could conclude that these types of aid flows should be exclusively channelled via NGOs, whereas the focus of bilateral donors should rather be assisting the domestic industry or implementing infrastructure projects. This follows from the fact that Masud and Yontcheva (2005: 13) find that only NGO aid proves to have a positive effect on infant mortality.

8 Conclusion

After 50 years of intensive research, scholars and theorists still have not reached a conclusion on aid effectiveness. Consequentially, the purpose of this study was to analyse whether or not aid contributes to globally established development goals. When looking at the aggregated aid effects - as measured by the impact on three development indicators, i.e. GDP growth per capita, infant mortality and primary completion -, the conclusion appeared negative – neither total bilateral aid nor total flows from multilateral agencies proved to have a positive impact on the chosen development indicators.

A detailed analysis of the aid allocation literature brought insight into the possible causes behind the failure of aggregated aid. Several previous studies find that the aid allocation of many major aid donors can largely be explained by determinants that are related to their own objectives, such as power-political interests, as measured by the UN voting pattern, or a high correlation with the donors' trading pattern. Some donor countries, however, are assumed to allocate aid with a high focus on both the needs of recipients and such factors that are supposed to increase the effectiveness of aid (i.e., quality of institutions or polices), rather than towards personal interest. Due to this finding, this study was aimed to compare the aid effectiveness between two groups of bilateral donors that purportedly allocate aid in a significantly different manner.

In a first step, a descriptive analysis confirmed the findings of the aid allocation in the case of the two chosen donor groups. This investigation provided the finding that G1 donors (Denmark, Finland, the Netherlands, Norway and Sweden) allocate most of their funds to LCDs that face high levels of infant mortality and low levels of GDP per capita as well as primary completion. G2 donors (France, Germany, Japan, the UK and the US), on the other hand, showed to direct substantial funds to recipient countries with an already further developed economy and significantly better social conditions, e.g. Egypt, Israel, Indonesia or China. A closer look at the individual allocation of each donor, moreover, confirmed the high role of personal interest for each G2 country; the preference for trading partners, formerly colonised or for geographically closer countries, as well as political motives appeared to be plausible explanations for the allocation patterns of those donors. In contrast, this could not be demonstrated for any of the G1 donors.

A further objective of this introductory investigation was to determine differences in donor-specific aid allocations between the pre- and post-Cold War era. It became apparent that donors of both groups have increasingly diversified their aid payments after 1989, whereas they had provided large shares of their aid budgets to only a few recipients in the period prior to that year. This could be a first indication for the lesser importance of strategic political relations to single recipient countries, as global political tensions had lightened with the end of the Cold War; additionally, it falls in line with previous findings of the literature.

A closer inspection of the individual choice of recipient countries made by each donor, however, showed that not much has changed after 1989. Although more LCDs are among the most preferred recipients of G2 aid during the post-Cold War period, this analysis demonstrated that individual G2 donors still transfer large budget shares to key recipients of potentially great political or economic importance. Examples for former colonised countries that remain important G2 recipients are Nigeria, India and Bangladesh in the case of the UK; or Cote d'Ivoire, Morocco, Senegal and Cameroon as those countries with the highest French aid receipts. Japan proved to still allocate most of its resources to China, India and countries in Southeast Asia; which could be explained due to political and economic interests in nearby countries. Egypt and Israel, moreover, showed to be the two main recipients of US aid after 1989 – because both countries are among the most important political allies of the US in the Middle East, this observation is consistent with the insight of previous studies; i.e. the pattern of US aid flows can largely be explained by political interests in this region. Finally, in the case of Germany as a donor, China and Egypt appear to have been the two key recipients during the period from 1990 onwards. Equal to the other G2 donors, political or economic interest are possible explanations for this.

Temporal changes in the selection of recipient by G1 donors proved to be small too, however, with the difference that economically less-developed countries determine the pattern of G1 aid allocation both during and after the Cold War. From 1990 onwards, G1 donors provide aid almost exclusively to LCDs, many of which are located in SSA. These differences in the way G1 and G2 distribute their funds led to the conclusion that the extent to which aid impacts the chosen development indicators may differ significantly. As observed, G2 flows account for more than four times of the aid from G1 donors; so, the evidence that both donor groups showed to allocate their funds significantly supported the assumption that potentially positive effects of G1 donors can be overlooked when analysing the effect of total bilateral flows. Since most of the previous research focuses on analysing the effects of total aggregated aid, this study aimed to investigate aid flows from individual donors separately.

The subsequent regression analysis could, for one part, clearly confirm this hypothesis. Among all estimations that deal with the effect on growth, G1 aid showed to have a significant and highly positive impact, whereas aid from G2 donors consistently appeared to be ineffective. This result has proved to be robust among all estimation methods, i.e. system and difference GMM methodology, further panel data analyses based on OLS and FE estimators, and the initial approximation with cross-sectional data. This should be seen against the background that, concerning the aid-growth investigation, regressions of this study took up the specification of Rajan and Subramanian (2008). The finding of this paper, which applies a broad range of estimations and which is commonly considered to apply a convincing strategy for measuring the impact of aid, is that aid and growth are generally uncorrelated. With the objective of providing the clearest possible evidence for the difference between G1 and G2 aid effectiveness, this study largely maintained the original specification of Rajan and Subramanian (2008).

The conclusion that G1 aid positively affects growth, while flows from presumably more self-interested bilateral donors do not, corresponds with the findings of Minoiu and Reddy (2010). A major difference in the procedure, however, is that this thesis directly compared two groups of five donors: five that are consistently reported to allocate aid fairly, and five that show a stronger orientation towards own objectives. This approach revealed clear differences between the two donor groups. In some observations, G2 aid even showed a moderately significant negative effect on growth. Furthermore, this study has strengthened the evidence that aid effectiveness can differ significantly between distinct donors on a broader and more specific empirical basis. First, the suggestions of Roodman (2009A: 128-129) to prevent instrument proliferation in order to reduce the measurement bias to a minimum was strictly followed by limiting the lags of the endogenous GMM-style variables and, additionally, by collapsing the instruments. This resulted in reasonably low p-values of the Hansen test among the system and difference GMM estimations. Minoiu and Reddy (2010: 36), in contrast, do not report the number of instruments applied to their estimations and mainly achieve Hansen p-values of 1.000. In addition, this study provided further evidence by additionally applying difference GMM, FE and OLS method the panel data.

A further objective was to identify the timing effects of aid, by allowing for lagged values of the respective variables. The decision to consider the possibility that aid effects arrive after a significantly large time period proved to be crucial. It appeared that G1 aid, which can be seen as a proxy for effective development assistance at this point, shows only weakly significant coefficients among the main GMM estimations when including a lag of five years, whereas the coefficients for all ten-year lagged G1 variables proved to be highly significant. Extending the lag for a further five years, however, resulted in a loss of significance. Since the best results came from G1 aid lagged ten years, and a five-year lag still had a certain explanatory power, the study concluded that aid largely affects growth within five to ten years. Considering that several previous studies argue that a large part of the aid impacts may arrive after a very long period, this is largely in line with the result of Clemens et al. (2012: 608), who determine a significant positive effect of early-impact aid. This observation, moreover, sharply contrasts the finding of Minoiu and Reddy (2010: 36), who identify a coefficient of more than 100 for G1 aid lagged 25 years. This difference regarding the most appropriate time lag might principally be explained by the above-mentioned reduction of the instruments applied in this thesis.

Previous aid allocation research, furthermore, suggests that several bilateral donors have changed aid distribution since the end of the Cold War. In order to determine whether these changes also result in higher aid effectiveness, this study ran additional regressions with an observation period limited to the past 25 years. G1 aid appeared to show (moderately) higher aid effectiveness when looking at the post-Cold War period. Neither G2 nor the coefficients for total MA and BA showed to be significantly positive. This contrasts with the results of Headey (2008: 172) and Bearce and Tirone (2010: 847), which both find a significantly positive change in effectiveness of total aid flows in their post-Cold War analyses. However, both studies apply a considerably different instrumentation strategy and, moreover, find a significantly positive effect of total aid when looking at the total observation period as opposed to this study. The insight that the (in)effectiveness of G2 aid, as well as of MA and BA, also applies to the post-Cold War period is in line with Harrigan and Wang (2011: 1290), who find that key variables capturing strategic motives behind the aid allocation of major donors do not change after 1989.

Several studies state that growth may not be the only conclusive factor for the analysis aid effectiveness; this motivated an additional investigation of the impact on two social indicators, i.e. infant mortality and primary completion. The resulting findings, however, could not confirm the positive effect of G1 aid; none of the conducted estimations provided a significantly positive impact of any of the aid variables. This proved to be consistent for both indicators, at all time lags, both full and limited observation period, as well as among all different estimation methods. One plausible explanation for this might be derived from Masud and Yontcheva (2005: 13), who also find total aid to be ineffective when estimating the impact on infant mortality, whereas they report significantly positive coefficients for aid provided by NGOs. Consequently, this study brought up the possible conclusion that bilateral and multilateral aid may be effective in promoting growth if implemented correctly, whereas the apparent ineffectiveness concerning the improvement of social conditions could indicate a lack of proximity to the poor population. This explanation refers to the fact that NGOs, in contrast to bilateral agencies, typically dedicate to helping the poorest. It is also in line with the conclusion of Chong et al. (2009: 79), who cannot determine a positive effect of total aid on poverty alleviation.

This conclusion, however, appears to contradict several other previous investigations of the aid effect on other social indicators, particularly concerning funds from multilateral donors. Alvi and Senbeta (2012: 968), for instance, find that MA significantly reduces poverty among recipient countries. Gomanee et al. (2005B: 306-307) observe that even total aid has a positive impact on the HDI and achieves to reduce infant mortality. Moreover, Dreher et al. (2008: 304-305) observe a positive and significant impact of education aid on primary school enrolment. Therefore, empirical shortcomings in the estimations of both indicators were stated as a further major explanation for the lack of significance among all coefficients for aid. First, a closer look on the results revealed that data availability for control variables of the social indicators estimations is considerably weaker than in the case of the growth analysis. This resulted in an observation number of the social indicator panel data estimations of less than compared to the growth chapter. Second, it needs to be acknowledged that aid research based on social outcomes is relatively novel compared to the established aid-growth field. Consequently, chosen estimation methods and the applied set of instruments might not be most accurate for determining aid effects.

Referring to the last-mentioned shortcomings, it is apparent that further aid research in the field of social indicators is needed, as soon as data availability in this area improves. Additionally, it is crucial to identify the best instrumentation strategy in order to estimate the effects of aid on parameters such as infant mortality or primary completion. The quality of data concerning social determinants in LCDs appears to be a major reason why previous research predominantly focuses on measuring the impact on growth. Still, social indicators are among the most important development objectives of the UN and; as discussed, there are reasons to assume that improvements in social areas do not have to necessarily impact growth in the end. Therefore, future research should urgently tackle the way how to measure the effect on social indicators in the most appropriate way, beside the consideration of economic growth.

The decision to form two groups of donors with a similar pattern of aid allocation, instead of analysing the aid effects of individual donor countries, was based on the advantage of a direct comparison with previous studies in the first place. In addition, this procedure holds the advantage that observed aid flows are considerably higher and, therefore, should achieve better empirical results. By examining the aid effectiveness of single donors, such as the US or Japan (with already high aid flows), one may uncover additional valuable insights. Furthermore, previous literature such as that of Harrigan and Wang (2011: 1290) finds differences in the aid allocation of donors that are included in the G2 variable of this study. A further improvement of empirical nature could be to explicitly test the assumption that aid affects government expenditures (of any kind). The insight that aid has a positive impact on health expenditures, for instance, or on military expenditures as a counterexample, could be of interest for research.

The aim of this thesis was to assess aid effects using existing observations provided by the aid allocation literature, while avoiding an extensive investigation of why different donors achieve substantially different results. In addition to the explanation derived from aid allocation studies, it is clear that there are several other causes behind the results of this study. For instance, this study does not include an aid-policy interaction term as it is applied by Burnside and Dollar (2000) among others. Such a procedure could additionally examine the role of institutional quality or sound policies of recipient countries when evaluating differences between donors. Moreover, one major strategic determinant derived by the aid allocation literature is the correlation between provided aid and the donors' exports, with the underlying assumption that aid can be used as a means of export promotion. Another useful extension to this study would be to analyse if aid from G2 donors eventually leads to increasing exports. One could also extend this to the correlation with other strategic parameters, such as improvements in political relations; however, it would certainly be more difficult to measure.

Further important evidence might, furthermore, be derived at the micro level. Detailed project analyses with the objective to determine major differences in project design or implementation between donors could provide further explanations for differences in effectiveness than strategic motives. As this study finds that most aid effects arrive after a period of five to ten years, whereas many studies do not consider lagged values of aid, evidence from an extensive project assessment could also give a clearer answer on which lag to apply for aid analysis on a macroeconomic level. If it turns out that most projects require several years after aid has been disbursed to achieve results, for instance, the use of non-lagged aid would have to be reconsidered.

Against the background that several recently emerged donors, such as China, Brazil or South Africa, account for increasingly higher funding, and so investigation of individual donors' aid effectiveness remains an important topic for future research. But regardless of which donor provides funds, aid should be aid and nothing else. As discussed, various other causes for the ineffectiveness for aid may emerge. However, if future research reinforces the evidence that individual interests are a main driver, the international community needs to take countermeasures; it may be the role of future researchers to initiate this process.

Appendix

Appendix A: *The UN Development Goals*

Millenium Development Goals (2000)

Goal 1	Eradicate extreme poverty and hunger
Goal 2	Achieve universal primary education
Goal 3	Promote gender equality and empower women
Goal 4	Reduce child mortality rates
Goal 5	Improve maternal health
Goal 6	Combat HIV/AIDS, malaria, and other diseases
Goal 7	Ensure environmental sustainability
Goal 8	Develop a global partnership for development

Sources: UNDP (2003).

Sustainable Development Goals (2016)

Goal 1	No Poverty
Goal 2	Zero Hunger
Goal 3	Good Health and Well-being
Goal 4	Quality Education
Goal 5	Gender Equality
Goal 6	Clean Water and Sanitation
Goal 7	Affordable and Clean Energy
Goal 8	Decent Work and Economic Growth
Goal 9	Industry, Innovation and Infrastructure
Goal 10	Reduced Inequalities
Goal 11	Sustainable Cities and Communities
Goal 12	Responsible Consumption and Production
Goal 13	Climate Action
Goal 14	Life Below Water
Goal 15	Life on Land
Goal 16	Peace, Justice and Strong Institutions
Goal 17	Partnerships for the Goals

Sources: DESA (2016).

Appendix B: *Data description and sources*

Appendix B1: Variable description and sources

Variable	Description	Source
	Dependent variables	
GDP per capita growth	Average annual growth rate of GDP per capita (PPP). Values are averaged over the relevant period. For cross-sectional estimations, total decrease rates over the whole observation period are included. For the panel data analysis.	World Bank (2016)
Infant Mortality rate	Mortality rate of infant per 1000 live births. For cross-sectional estimations, total decrease rates over the whole observation period are included. The natural logarithm of five-year averages are included in the panel data.	
Primary completion rate	In percent of the total relevant age group of the population. For cross-sectional estimations, total increase rates over the whole observation period are included. The natural logarithms of five-year averages are taken in the panel data.	
	Aid variables	
Total bilateral aid (BA)	ODA from all bilateral DAC countries as % of the GNI. Averages are taken for each relevant observation period.	OECD-DAC (2016)
Total multilateral aid (MA)	ODA from all multilateral donors listed in OECD-DAC countries as % of the GNI. These include UN-institution, international and regional development banks, EU institutions, the IMF; the World Bank Group and other multilateral donors. Averages are taken for each relevant observation period.	
Group 1 aid (G1 aid)	ODA from Denmark, Finland, the Netherlands, Norway and Sweden. Averages are taken for each relevant observation period.	
Group 2 aid (G2 aid)	ODA from France, Germany, Japan, the Uk and the US. Averages are taken for each relevant observation period.	
Aid from all non-Group 1 donors (n. G1 aid)	ODA from all other donors than from G1 countries. Averages are taken for each relevant observation period.	
Aid from all non-Group 2 donors	ODA from all other donors than from G2 countries. Averages are taken for each relevant observation period.	
	Controll variables: All estimations	
Initial income	Natural logarithm of the GDP per capita in constant 2010 USD at the beginning of each relevant observation period.	World Bank (2016)
Institutional quality	Summary index of the Fraser Institute measure for economic freedom. This includes indices in the areas size of government, legal system and property rights, sound money, freedom to trade internationally and regulation. Averages are taken for each relevant observation period.	Gwartney et al. (2016)
Political instability	Summary index of the INSCR database for Major Episodes of Political Violence. This includes magnitude scores in national and international warfare that a recipient country is affected with. Averages are taken for each relevant observation period.	Marshall (2016)
	Controll variables: Growth estimations	
Initial life expectancy	Natural logarithm of life expectancy at birth at the beginning of each relevant observation period.	World Bank (2016)
Geography	Average of number of frost days and tropical land area.	Rajan and Subramanian (2008)
Budget balance	In percent of the GDP. Averages are included for each relevant period.	World Bank (2016)
Initial policy	Only included in cross-sectional estimations. Observation periods with a beginning of earlier than 1990 apply the openness index by Sachs and Warner (1995), all later periods use the updated index by Wacziarg and Welch (2008).	Sachs and Warner (1995), Wacziarg and Welch (2008)
Trade to GDP	Trade volume as percent of GDP. Only included in panel data estimations. Averages are taken over each relevant period.	World Bank (2016)
Inflation	Annual inflation as measured by consumer prices. Averages are taken over each relevant period.	World Bank (2016)
	Controll variables: Social indicators estimations	
Health expenditures	Public health expenditures in percent of the GDP. Averages are taken over each relevant period.	World Bank (2016)
Education expenditures	Public education expenditures in percent of the GDP. Averages are taken over each relevant period.	
Urbanisation	Natural logarithm of the urbanised share of the population. Averages are taken over each relevant period.	
Poverty	Poverty headcount at USD 1.9 per day. Averages are taken over each relevant period.	
Population growth	Annual population growth. Averages are taken over each relevant period.	

Code	Country Name	Dummy	Code	Country Name	Dummy	Code	Country Name	Dummy
ALB	Albania		FJI	Fiji	East Asia	NAM	Namibia	SSA
DZA	Algeria		GAB	Gabon	SSA	NPL	Nepal	
AGO	Angola	SSA	GMB	Gambia, The	SSA	NIC	Nicaragua	
ARG	Argentina		GEO	Georgia		NER	Niger	SSA
ARM	Armenia		GHA	Ghana	SSA	NGA	Nigeria	SSA
AZE	Azerbaijan		GTM	Guatemala		PAK	Pakistan	
BGD	Bangladesh		GIN	Guinea	SSA	PAN	Panama	
BLZ	Belize		GNB	GuineaBissau	SSA	PNG	Papua New Guinea	East Asia
BEN	Benin	SSA	HTI	Haiti		PRY	Paraguay	
BOL	Bolivia		HND	Honduras		PER	Peru	
BWA	Botswana	SSA	IND	India		PHL	Philippines	East Asia
BRA	Brazil		IDN	Indonesia	East Asia	RWA	Rwanda	SSA
BFA	Burkina Faso	SSA	IRN	Iran, Islamic Rep.		SEN	Senegal	SSA
BDI	Burundi	SSA	ISR	Israel		SLE	Sierra Leone	SSA
CMR	Cameroon	SSA	JAM	Jamaica		SGP	Singapore	East Asia
CPV	Cape Verde	SSA	JOR	Jordan		SVN	Slovenia	
CAF	Central African Rep.	SSA	KAZ	Kazakhstan		ZAF	South Africa	SSA
TCD	Chad	SSA	KEN	Kenya	SSA	LKA	Sri Lanka	
CHL	Chile		KOR	Korea, Rep.	East Asia	SWZ	Swaziland	SSA
CHN	China	East Asia	KGZ	Kyrgyz Republic		SYR	Syrian Arab Republic	
COL	Colombia		LBN	Lebanon		TZA	Tanzania	SSA
COM	Comoros	SSA	LSO	Lesotho	SSA	THA	Thailand	East Asia
ZAR	Congo, Dem. Rep.	SSA	MKD	Macedonia, FYR		TGO	Togo	SSA
COG	Congo, Rep.	SSA	MDG	Madagascar	SSA	TTO	Trinidad & Tobago	
CRI	Costa Rica		MWI	Malawi	SSA	TUN	Tunisia	
CIV	Cote d'Ivoire	SSA	MYS	Malaysia	East Asia	TUR	Turkey	
HRV	Croatia		MLI	Mali	SSA	UGA	Uganda	SSA
DOM	Dominican Republic		MRT	Mauritania	SSA	UKR	Ukraine	
ECU	Ecuador		MUS	Mauritius	SSA	URY	Uruguay	
EGY	Egypt, Arab Rep.		MEX	Mexico		VEN	Venezuela, RB	
SLV	El Salvador		MDA	Moldova		YEM	Yemen, Rep.	
GNQ	Equatorial Guinea		MAR	Morocco		ZMB	Zambia	SSA
ETH	Ethiopia	SSA	MOZ	Mozambique	SSA	ZWE	Zimbabwe	SSA

Notes: The table shows all recipient countries (groups) of the cross-section and panel data analyses. Dummies for Sub-Saharan Africa (SSA) and East Asia are from Minoiu and Reddy (2010).

Appendix C: *Patterns of aid allocation*

Appendix C1: Development of aid payments by individual donors

	1960-1964	1965-1969	1970-1974	1975-1979	1980-1984	Period 1985-1989	1990-1994	1995-1999	2000-2004	2004-2009	2010-2014
Dänermark	0.01	0.07	0.28	0.85	1.14	2.05	3.70	5.00	5.33	8.21	10.44
Finnland	0.00	0.00	0.04	0.15	0.43	1.39	1.96	1.08	1.40	3.12	4.23
Niederlande	0.15	0.32	1.03	3.33	5.13	6.42	8.95	10.95	12.42	22.61	20.71
Norwegen	0.01	0.04	0.18	0.81	1.51	2.46	3.79	4.72	6.02	13.33	18.64
Schweden	0.03	0.14	0.62	2.38	2.96	4.56	7.32	5.98	7.57	14.19	18.48
Frankreich	4.15	3.14	3.87	6.70	11.49	18.20	30.45	25.27	19.82	35.27	37.79
Deutschland	1.73	2.14	3.40	7.00	10.80	14.06	23.09	19.76	16.75	38.59	46.40
Japan	0.49	1.45	2.93	6.00	11.49	24.74	41.64	44.21	36.17	36.42	35.45
UK	1.93	2.05	2.29	3.76	5.26	5.77	8.28	9.86	18.03	37.22	46.93
USA	15.99	15.81	13.11	16.21	25.56	36.53	40.24	30.31	57.17	114.27	132.50
Other bilateral DAC donors	1.19	2.50	4.42	7.76	12.91	24.04	35.07	28.49	36.76	82.13	90.48
MA donors	1.05	3.79	8.13	23.29	36.73	47.86	78.36	79.15	87.16	147.38	201.39

Notes: Data from OECD-DAC.

Appendix C2: *Aid allocation of individual G1 donors*

Denmark

	1960-1989				1990 - 2014		
Recipient	Share of aid	GDP per capita	Infant Mortality	Recipient	Share of aid	GDP per capita	Infant Mortality
Tanzania	15.27%	475.08	120.03	Tanzania	6.71%	590.44	69.04
India	9.68%	399.56	127.98	Uganda	4.67%	476.53	76.30
Bangladesh	8.49%	371.65	140.29	Mozambique	4.55%	309.04	105.59
Kenya	7.31%	751.22	82.16	Ghana	3.75%	1123.29	60.95
Mozambique	3.17%	158.75	175.95	Bangladesh	3.41%	601.66	60.10
Egypt, Arab Rep.	2.65%	1075.31	136.11	Kenya	2.48%	921.34	57.12
China	2.20%	319.27	55.54	Burkina Faso	2.37%	469.07	86.88
Zimbabwe	1.88%	1100.75	68.81	Zambia	2.32%	1149.42	81.14
Malawi	1.75%	338.71	176.75	Nepal	2.14%	495.89	56.53
Zambia	1.68%	1391.76	106.04	Nicaragua	1.91%	1378.95	31.50

Finland

	1960-1989				1990 - 2014		
Recipient	Share of aid	GDP per capita	Infant Mortality	Recipient	Share of aid	GDP per capita	Infant Mortality
Tanzania	17.92%	475.08	120.03	Tanzania	5.94%	590.44	69.04
Zambia	8.76%	1391.76	106.04	Mozambique	4.95%	309.04	105.59
Kenya	6.42%	751.22	82.16	Zambia	3.22%	1149.42	81.14
Mozambique	4.71%	158.75	175.95	Kenya	3.19%	921.34	57.12
Egypt, Arab Rep.	4.66%	1075.31	136.11	Ethiopia	2.85%	258.53	79.45
Sri Lanka	4.03%	827.08	45.24	Nepal	2.80%	495.89	56.53
Ethiopia	3.48%	216.50	138.89	Nicaragua	2.30%	1378.95	31.50
Nicaragua	2.96%	1922.23	95.90	China	1.98%	2768.01	25.52
Bangladesh	2.71%	371.65	140.29	Namibia	1.48%	4369.62	44.13
Nepal	2.42%	293.54	159.78	Egypt, Arab Rep.	1.16%	2124.61	36.37

The Netherlands

	1960-1989				1990 - 2014		
Recipient	Share of aid	GDP per capita	Infant Mortality	Recipient	Share of aid	GDP per capita	Infant Mortality
Indonesia	10.15%	910.50	100.78	Tanzania	2.45%	590.44	69.04
India	8.86%	399.56	127.98	Bangladesh	2.09%	601.66	60.10
Tanzania	5.20%	475.08	120.03	Mozambique	1.94%	309.04	105.59
Bangladesh	4.66%	371.65	140.29	Ghana	1.85%	1123.29	60.95
Kenya	3.32%	751.22	82.16	Ethiopia	1.71%	258.53	79.45
Pakistan	2.33%	505.97	135.32	Congo, Dem. Rep.	1.58%	349.78	100.02
Mozambique	2.01%	158.75	175.95	Mali	1.54%	530.73	104.42
Sri Lanka	1.94%	827.08	45.24	Bolivia	1.43%	1742.74	54.49
Peru	1.93%	3374.03	93.50	Indonesia	1.39%	2560.52	39.08
Burkina Faso	1.72%	288.67	132.79	Burkina Faso	1.37%	469.07	86.88

Norway

	1960-1989				1990 - 2014		
Recipient	Share of aid	GDP per capita	Infant Mortality	Recipient	Share of aid	GDP per capita	Infant Mortality
Tanzania	14.31%	475.08	120.03	Tanzania	4.04%	590.44	69.04
Bangladesh	7.60%	371.65	140.29	Mozambique	3.30%	309.04	105.59
India	7.02%	399.56	127.98	Brazil	2.63%	9467.25	27.03
Kenya	6.75%	751.22	82.16	Zambia	2.45%	1149.42	81.14
Mozambique	5.62%	158.75	175.95	Uganda	2.11%	476.53	76.30
Zambia	5.23%	1391.76	106.04	Malawi	1.78%	401.97	89.06
Pakistan	3.56%	505.97	135.32	Ethiopia	1.70%	258.53	79.45
Botswana	3.25%	1482.48	71.55	Bangladesh	1.43%	601.66	60.10
Sri Lanka	2.87%	827.08	45.24	Sri Lanka	1.27%	2144.60	13.32
Zimbabwe	2.60%	1100.75	68.81	Nepal	1.20%	495.89	56.53

Sweden

	1960-1989				1990 - 2014		
Recipient	Share of aid	GDP per capita	Infant Mortality	Recipient	Share of aid	GDP per capita	Infant Mortality
Tanzania	11.39%	475.08	120.03	Tanzania	4.04%	590.44	69.04
India	10.59%	399.56	127.98	Mozambique	3.88%	309.04	105.59
Mozambique	6.02%	158.75	175.95	Congo, Dem. Rep.	1.90%	349.78	100.02
Ethiopia	3.98%	216.50	138.89	Ethiopia	1.75%	258.53	79.45
Bangladesh	3.90%	371.65	140.29	Kenya	1.74%	921.34	57.12
Zambia	3.77%	1391.76	106.04	Zambia	1.67%	1149.42	81.14
Kenya	3.33%	751.22	82.16	Uganda	1.63%	476.53	76.30
Sri Lanka	2.92%	827.08	45.24	Bangladesh	1.49%	601.66	60.10
Angola	2.30%	2909.80	135.47	Nicaragua	1.41%	1378.95	31.50
Nicaragua	2.03%	1922.23	95.90	India	1.30%	996.81	61.79

Notes: Data from OECD-DAC and WDI. The table shows only the recipient countries of the sample (see Appendix B2). Additional countries with high aid receipts might be omitted.

Appendix C3: *Aid allocation of individual G2 donors*

France

Recipient	1960-1989 Share of aid	GDP per capita	Infant Mortality	Recipient	1990 - 2014 Share of aid	GDP per capita	Infant Mortality
Algeria	7.14%	3025.78	113.41	Cote d'Ivoire	5.58%	1315.23	91.04
Morocco	4.64%	1248.95	106.60	Morocco	4.45%	2315.58	40.10
Senegal	4.09%	959.87	104.58	Senegal	3.47%	911.69	59.48
Cote d'Ivoire	3.66%	1792.29	141.76	Cameroon	3.24%	1115.32	79.92
Cameroon	2.61%	1111.82	119.55	Egypt, Arab Rep.	3.08%	2124.61	36.37
Madagascar	2.45%	628.15	101.84	Congo, Rep.	2.69%	2692.18	58.97
Tunisia	2.33%	1721.57	98.39	Nigeria	2.53%	1726.06	102.19
Mali	2.05%	304.51	174.96	China	2.25%	2768.01	25.52
Congo, Rep.	1.89%	2141.92	80.87	Algeria	2.24%	3916.91	30.59
Central African Republic	1.88%	571.25	131.07	Congo, Dem. Rep.	2.13%	349.78	100.02

Germany

Recipient	1960-1989 Share of aid	GDP per capita	Infant Mortality	Recipient	1990 - 2014 Share of aid	GDP per capita	Infant Mortality
India	6.41%	399.56	127.98	China	5.36%	2768.01	25.52
Turkey	6.03%	4587.36	108.43	Egypt, Arab Rep.	3.27%	2124.61	36.37
Egypt, Arab Rep.	4.63%	1075.31	136.11	India	2.72%	996.81	61.79
Indonesia	3.77%	910.50	100.78	Nigeria	2.36%	1726.06	102.19
Israel	3.68%	14820.51	15.31	Cameroon	2.04%	1115.32	79.92
Bangladesh	2.90%	371.65	140.29	Brazil	1.70%	9467.25	27.03
Pakistan	2.85%	505.97	135.32	Congo, Dem. Rep.	1.60%	349.78	100.02
Brazil	2.54%	6124.09	88.91	Zambia	1.35%	1149.42	81.14
Tanzania	2.09%	475.08	120.03	Ethiopia	1.30%	258.53	79.45
Peru	1.84%	3374.03	93.50	Tanzania	1.22%	590.44	69.04

Japan

Recipient	1960-1989 Share of aid	GDP per capita	Infant Mortality	Recipient	1990 - 2014 Share of aid	GDP per capita	Infant Mortality
Indonesia	14.11%	910.50	100.78	China	7.11%	2768.01	25.52
China	8.68%	319.27	55.54	India	6.25%	996.81	61.79
Philippines	7.90%	1393.74	54.57	Indonesia	5.14%	2560.52	39.08
Thailand	6.95%	1193.08	60.99	Philippines	3.05%	1825.65	29.43
Bangladesh	5.86%	371.65	140.29	Pakistan	2.76%	923.91	84.88
India	4.38%	399.56	127.98	Sri Lanka	2.12%	2144.60	13.32
Pakistan	4.02%	505.97	135.32	Bangladesh	1.87%	601.66	60.10
Korea, Rep.	3.41%	3389.76	30.99	Tanzania	1.62%	590.44	69.04
Malaysia	3.04%	2674.18	35.63	Thailand	1.28%	4101.51	18.17
Egypt, Arab Rep.	2.85%	1075.31	136.11	Kenya	1.13%	921.34	57.12

UK

Recipient	1960-1989 Share of aid	GDP per capita	Infant Mortality	Recipient	1990 - 2014 Share of aid	GDP per capita	Infant Mortality
India	15.90%	399.56	127.98	Nigeria	6.69%	1726.06	102.19
Kenya	5.20%	751.22	82.16	India	6.56%	996.81	61.79
Bangladesh	4.21%	371.65	140.29	Bangladesh	3.72%	601.66	60.10
Pakistan	3.39%	505.97	135.32	Ethiopia	3.43%	258.53	79.45
Tanzania	3.36%	475.08	120.03	Tanzania	3.34%	590.44	69.04
Zambia	3.08%	1391.76	106.04	Pakistan	2.99%	923.91	84.88
Malawi	3.05%	338.71	176.75	Uganda	2.13%	476.53	76.30
Sri Lanka	2.35%	827.08	45.24	Ghana	2.12%	1123.29	60.95
Nigeria	1.87%	1550.67	147.53	Congo, Dem. Rep.	2.11%	349.78	100.02
Ghana	1.76%	939.29	108.73	Malawi	1.94%	401.97	89.06

US

Recipient	1960-1989 Share of aid	GDP per capita	Infant Mortality	Recipient	1990 - 2014 Share of aid	GDP per capita	Infant Mortality
Israel	13.50%	14820.51	15.31	Egypt, Arab Rep.	4.48%	2124.61	36.37
Egypt, Arab Rep.	10.56%	1075.31	136.11	Israel	2.54%	26931.89	5.48
India	7.31%	399.56	127.98	Ethiopia	2.26%	258.53	79.45
Pakistan	4.46%	505.97	135.32	Pakistan	2.12%	923.91	84.88
Korea, Rep.	2.40%	3389.76	30.99	Jordan	2.00%	3364.01	22.03
Bangladesh	2.25%	371.65	140.29	Colombia	1.74%	5435.18	20.36
Indonesia	2.19%	910.50	100.78	Kenya	1.72%	921.34	57.12
Turkey	2.10%	4587.36	108.43	Congo, Dem. Rep.	1.58%	349.78	100.02
El Salvador	2.01%	2493.38	90.49	Haiti	1.55%	718.02	73.82
Philippines	1.82%	1393.74	54.57	South Africa	1.34%	6648.04	46.60

Notes: Data from OECD-DAC and WDI. The table shows only the recipient countries of the sample (see Appendix B2). Additional countries with high aid receipts might be omitted.

Appendix D: *Cross-sectional estimation results*

Appendix D1: *Alternative estimation results without considering total aid flows*

	Dependent variable: Average annual growth rate in 1990-2015	
	(2)	(3)
G1 aid 1960-1999	23.94	
	(22.25)	
G2 aid 1960-1999		-26.27**
		(11.71)
Initial Income	-0.574	-0.777**
	(0.352)	(0.331)
Initial life expectancy	3.049	2.294
	(2.053)	(1.919)
Institutional quality	0.757***	0.737***
	(0.281)	(0.235)
Geography	0.522**	0.473**
	(0.254)	(0.231)
Budget balance	0.0347	0.00762
	(0.0427)	(0.0400)
Political instability	0.192**	0.0759
	(0.0899)	(0.0964)
Initial policy	-0.474	-0.408
	(0.371)	(0.349)
Inflation	-0.00191***	-0.00227***
	(0.000469)	(0.000499)
Constant	-10.35*	-4.915
	(5.984)	(6.256)
Observations	73	73
R-squared	0.445	0.473

Sources: Author's calculations.
Notes: The dependent variable is the average GDP growth rate during the period 1990-2004. Robust standard errors in parentheses. For descriptions of the variables and their sources, see appendix B1. The variables N-G1 and N-G2 for measuring the influence of total remaining aid as addition to the two group aid variables are omitted in both specifications. ***, ** and * denote statistical significance at the 1%, 5%, and 10% level respectively.

Appendix D2: *Aid 1970-1989, Growth 1990-2004*

	Dependent variable: Average annual growth rate in 1990-2004		
	(1)	(2)	(3)
BA 1970-1989	-9.730		
	(7.720)		
MA 1970-1989	-1.783		
	(22.89)		
G1 aid 1970-1989		22.47*	
		(11.33)	
Non G1 aid 1970-1989		-12.32***	
		(4.092)	
G2 aid 1970-1989			-17.05
			(14.99)
Non G2 aid 1970-1989			-5.127
			(5.447)
Initial Income	-0.550	-0.626*	-0.586
	(0.418)	(0.369)	(0.374)
Initial life expectancy	2.135	1.270	1.967
	(2.429)	(2.278)	(2.286)
Institutional quality	0.743*	0.939***	0.771**
	(0.385)	(0.322)	(0.324)
Geography	0.830***	0.879***	0.861***
	(0.250)	(0.241)	(0.247)
Budget balance	0.0618	0.0825*	0.0474
	(0.0477)	(0.0479)	(0.0460)
Political instability	0.0691	0.0568	0.0542
	(0.0804)	(0.0776)	(0.0782)
Initial policy	-0.505	-0.495	-0.503
	(0.445)	(0.402)	(0.421)
Inflation	0.000889	0.000802	0.000450
	(0.00104)	(0.000952)	(0.00102)
Constant	-6.283	-3.052	-5.282
	(7.510)	(6.884)	(7.059)
Observations	61	61	61
R-squared	0.488	0.539	0.507

Sources: Author's calculations.
Notes: The dependent variable is the average GDP growth rate during the period 1990-2004. Robust standard errors in parentheses. For descriptions of the variables and their sources, see appendix B1. ***, ** and * denote statistical significance at the 1%, 5%, and 10% level respectively.

Appendix D3: *Aid 1980-1999, Growth 1990-2004*

| | Dependent variable: Average annual growth rate in 1990-2004 | | |
	(1)	(2)	(3)
BA 1980-1999	**-4.675**		
	(9.710)		
MA 1980-1999	**2.199**		
	(17.69)		
G1 aid 1980-1999		**42.66****	
		(16.72)	
Non G1 aid 1980-1999		-12.52**	
		(5.504)	
G2 aid 1980-1999			**-20.24**
			(13.37)
Non G2 aid 1980-1999			0.787
			(3.778)
Initial Income	-0.462	-0.579	-0.505
	(0.392)	(0.373)	(0.383)
Initial life expectancy	2.415	0.772	1.628
	(2.526)	(2.323)	(2.429)
Institutional quality	0.756*	0.875**	0.800**
	(0.378)	(0.331)	(0.344)
Geography	0.844***	0.820***	0.796***
	(0.281)	(0.246)	(0.269)
Budget balance	0.0601	0.0699	0.0249
	(0.0576)	(0.0549)	(0.0581)
Political instability	0.0888	0.0615	0.0659
	(0.0738)	(0.0781)	(0.0791)
Initial policy	-0.521	-0.522	-0.597
	(0.415)	(0.398)	(0.417)
Inflation	0.00119	0.000298	0.000704
	(0.00114)	(0.000919)	(0.00116)
Constant	-8.406	-1.034	-4.778
	(8.219)	(7.216)	(7.549)
Observations	61	61	61
R-squared	0.469	0.527	0.488

Sources: Author's calculations.
Notes: The dependent variable is the average GDP growth rate during the period 1990-2004. Robust standard errors in parentheses. For descriptions of the variables and their sources, see appendix B1. ***, ** and * denote statistical significance at the 1%, 5%, and 10% level respectively.

Appendix D4: *Aid 1980-1999, Growth 2000-2014*

| | Dependent variable: Average annual growth rate in 1990-2014 | | |
	(1)	(2)	(3)
BA 1980-1999	**3.545**		
	(7.368)		
MA 1980-1999	**-10.06**		
	(11.99)		
G1 aid 1980-1999		**31.05***	
		(16.03)	
Non G1 aid 1980-1999		-10.13*	
		(5.597)	
G2 aid 1980-1999			**-20.55**
			(13.68)
Non G2 aid 1980-1999			3.226
			(4.341)
Initial Income	-0.455	-0.522	-0.454
	(0.329)	(0.330)	(0.324)
Initial life expectancy	0.565	0.619	0.479
	(1.648)	(1.537)	(1.531)
Institutional quality	0.425*	0.361	0.416*
	(0.230)	(0.228)	(0.234)
Geography	0.404	0.364	0.308
	(0.337)	(0.314)	(0.323)
Budget balance	0.0427	0.0287	0.0275
	(0.0301)	(0.0314)	(0.0320)
Political instability	0.139	0.100	0.103
	(0.131)	(0.131)	(0.133)
Initial policy	-0.371	-0.424	-0.422
	(0.387)	(0.384)	(0.387)
Inflation	-0.00438	-0.0105	-0.0113
	(0.0212)	(0.0200)	(0.0200)
Constant	1.388	2.444	2.122
	(5.439)	(4.996)	(4.906)
Observations	78	78	78
R-squared	0.142	0.186	0.165

Sources: Author's calculations.
Notes: The dependent variable is the average GDP growth rate during the period 2000-2014. Robust standard errors in parentheses. For descriptions of the variables and their sources, see appendix B1. ***, ** and * denote statistical significance at the 1%, 5%, and 10% level respectively.

	Dependent variable: Average annual growth rate in 1990-2014		
	(1)	(2)	(3)
BA 1990-2009	**9.125**		
	(9.130)		
MA 1990-2009	**-10.09**		
	(14.38)		
G1 aid 1990-2009		66.06***	
		(18.78)	
Non G1 aid 1990-2009		-11.37*	
		(6.044)	
G2 aid 1990-2009			**-5.286**
			(13.21)
Non G2 aid 1990-2009			3.363
			(6.402)
Initial Income	-0.379	-0.441	-0.377
	(0.337)	(0.327)	(0.343)
Initial life expectancy	0.833	0.748	0.913
	(1.751)	(1.633)	(1.602)
Institutional quality	0.466**	0.276	0.454*
	(0.220)	(0.235)	(0.229)
Geography	0.435	0.352	0.401
	(0.341)	(0.322)	(0.336)
Budget balance	0.0494	0.0390	0.0475
	(0.0324)	(0.0327)	(0.0315)
Political instability	0.169	0.133	0.158
	(0.132)	(0.126)	(0.134)
Initial policy	-0.440	-0.438	-0.425
	(0.384)	(0.370)	(0.394)
Inflation	-0.00267	-0.00955	-0.00270
	(0.0214)	(0.0180)	(0.0200)
Constant	-0.726	1.660	-0.933
	(5.972)	(5.620)	(5.381)
Observations	78	78	78
R-squared	0.147	0.218	0.138

Sources: Author's calculations.
Notes: The dependent variable is the average GDP growth rate during the period 1990-2004. Robust standard errors in parentheses. For descriptions of the variables and their sources, see appendix B1. ***, ** and * denote statistical significance at the 1%, 5%, and 10% level respectively.

Appendix E: *GMM estimation results: Aid and growth*

Appendix E1: *Whole period*

	Dependent variable: Average annual gdp growth per capita								
	(1)	(2)	(3)	(4)	(5)	(6)	(7)	(8)	(9)
G1 aid	**48.56***			**47.36***			**24.05**		
	(27.24)			(17.52)			(24.13)		
Non G1 aid	5.472			-4.177			-3.246		
	(9.812)			(7.228)			(8.917)		
G2 aid		**4.095**			**7.575**			**-17.43**	
		(24.19)			(18.25)			(19.79)	
Non G2 aid		18.98**			7.655			7.526	
		(9.433)			(7.585)			(7.391)	
BA			**0.728**			**7.605**			**-6.770**
			(11.31)			(10.49)			(7.795)
MA			**42.76***			**7.904**			**16.26**
			(23.74)			(18.22)			(19.57)
Initial Income	-2.582***	-1.951**	-1.217	-2.241**	-1.844*	-1.830	-2.168*	-2.059*	-2.202*
	(0.943)	(0.774)	(0.764)	(0.916)	(0.942)	(1.118)	(1.242)	(1.090)	(1.284)
Initial life expectancy	7.748	7.525	8.408	7.629	6.717	6.217	9.807*	5.664	6.391
	(5.238)	(5.417)	(5.434)	(5.209)	(5.710)	(6.531)	(5.831)	(5.784)	(6.662)
Geography	2.195***	2.143***	1.926***	1.623***	1.852***	1.697***	1.706**	1.826**	1.800**
	(0.746)	(0.665)	(0.546)	(0.608)	(0.644)	(0.603)	(0.715)	(0.789)	(0.707)
Institutional quality	1.064***	1.286***	1.026**	1.062**	1.068*	1.014*	0.913	1.263**	0.994
	(0.402)	(0.487)	(0.515)	(0.411)	(0.544)	(0.568)	(0.662)	(0.603)	(0.639)
Budget balance	0.164	0.119	0.106	0.143	0.128	0.172**	0.0828	0.104	0.132
	(0.124)	(0.106)	(0.0874)	(0.0983)	(0.0974)	(0.0854)	(0.121)	(0.102)	(0.118)
Political instability	0.00820	0.0913	0.115	-0.00984	0.0294	0.00364	0.0223	0.0748	0.0314
	(0.196)	(0.193)	(0.200)	(0.162)	(0.181)	(0.192)	(0.204)	(0.201)	(0.206)
Trade to GDP	4.704**	4.844**	4.631***	3.448**	4.254**	4.128***	5.010**	4.190**	4.323**
	(1.802)	(1.933)	(1.635)	(1.568)	(1.655)	(1.496)	(2.293)	(1.919)	(1.834)
Inflation	-0.000394	-0.000201	-0.000515	-3.83e-05	0.000221	0.000498	-0.000806	-0.000416	-0.000506
	(0.00164)	(0.00148)	(0.00134)	(0.00121)	(0.00133)	(0.00119)	(0.00164)	(0.00120)	(0.00146)
Constant	-35.19*	-41.71*	-48.97**	-31.91*	-35.19	-32.07	-47.39**	-29.60	-30.41
	(20.53)	(21.94)	(21.73)	(18.99)	(21.46)	(21.05)	(19.50)	(21.07)	(21.53)
Observations	526	526	526	526	526	526	526	526	526
No. of recipient countries	82	82	82	82	82	82	82	82	82
No. of instruments	56	56	56	56	56	56	56	56	56
Hansen test p-value	0.466	0.694	0.636	0.409	0.609	0.510	0.170	0.605	0.546
AR(2)	0.862	0.739	0.772	0.865	0.686	0.794	0.693	0.829	0.742

Sources: Author's calculations.
Notes: The dependent variable is the average annual growth rate of GDP per capita. Robust standard errors in parentheses. For descriptions of the variables and their sources, see appendix B1. ***, ** and * denote statistical significance at the 1%, 5%, and 10% level respectively.

Appendix E2: *Post-Cold War period*

	(1)	(2)	(3)	(4)	(5)	(6)	(7)	(8)	(9)
	Dependent variable: Average annual gdp growth per capita								
G1 aid	54.32**			37.81***			20.96		
	(23.74)			(13.40)			(19.85)		
Non G1 aid	-1.566			-5.165			-2.997		
	(8.841)			(5.257)			(6.564)		
G2 aid		-11.84			8.153			-26.62	
		(20.04)			(18.05)			(20.07)	
Non G2 aid		19.36**			11.49			8.959	
		(9.683)			(9.749)			(6.607)	
BA			-0.850			9.502			7.675
			(14.40)			(9.720)			(11.75)
MA			9.795			3.753			-12.24
			(25.54)			(26.02)			(19.76)
Initial Income	-1.114	-1.186	-0.850	-1.646**	-0.748	-1.000	-1.335	-1.337	-1.600**
	(1.053)	(0.771)	(0.920)	(0.744)	(0.882)	(0.942)	(0.888)	(0.842)	(0.774)
Initial life expectancy	3.330	4.716*	4.863	4.395	5.391*	4.791	5.338*	5.836**	3.914
	(2.708)	(2.771)	(3.283)	(3.129)	(2.922)	(3.019)	(2.918)	(2.674)	(3.216)
Geography	0.789	1.123	0.619	0.996	0.787	0.898*	0.975	0.743	1.153*
	(0.737)	(0.679)	(0.609)	(0.642)	(0.615)	(0.496)	(0.654)	(0.619)	(0.613)
Institutional quality	1.047***	1.180***	1.178***	1.159***	1.138***	1.229***	1.171***	1.138***	1.292**
	(0.395)	(0.358)	(0.415)	(0.295)	(0.372)	(0.376)	(0.438)	(0.424)	(0.497)
Budget balance	0.0794	0.0692	0.0751	0.0891	0.0620	0.0853	0.0503	0.0478	0.0943
	(0.0753)	(0.0622)	(0.0776)	(0.0654)	(0.0678)	(0.0586)	(0.0662)	(0.0585)	(0.0659)
Political instability	0.0288	0.0490	0.0973	0.0385	0.0667	0.0123	0.0967	0.109	0.0631
	(0.205)	(0.207)	(0.236)	(0.198)	(0.218)	(0.215)	(0.221)	(0.229)	(0.221)
Trade to GDP	1.619	2.068*	1.452	2.016*	2.090*	2.094*	2.446	2.162*	2.202
	(1.186)	(1.113)	(1.239)	(1.187)	(1.231)	(1.136)	(1.543)	(1.170)	(1.372)
Inflation	0.000381	0.000894	0.000915	0.000789	0.00127	0.00130	0.000744	0.000555	0.000922
	(0.00133)	(0.00112)	(0.00130)	(0.00105)	(0.00121)	(0.00120)	(0.00103)	(0.00119)	(0.00119)
Constant	-15.86	-23.89*	-24.65	-18.06	-30.40**	-26.19*	-26.55**	-27.16**	-18.01
	(14.05)	(12.29)	(16.64)	(12.94)	(14.95)	(14.00)	(12.45)	(11.22)	(13.53)
Observations	350	350	350	350	350	350	350	350	350
No. of recipient countries	82	82	82	82	82	82	82	82	82
No. of instruments	52	52	52	52	52	52	52	52	52
Hansen test p-value	0.645	0.629	0.239	0.534	0.674	0.776	0.656	0.684	0.678
AR(2)	0.657	0.774	0.936	0.863	0.929	0.985	0.942	0.589	0.859

Sources: Author's calculations.
Notes: The dependent variable is the average annual growth rate of GDP per capita with the observation period changed to 1990-2014. Robust standard errors in parentheses. For descriptions of the variables and their sources, see appendix B1. ***, ** and * denote statistical significance at the 1%, 5%, and 10% level respectively.

Appendix F: *GMM estimation results: Aid and social indicators*

Appendix F1: *The infant mortality regressions*

	(1)	(2)	(3)	(4)	(5)	(6)	(7)	(8)	(9)
				Dependent variable: Infant Mortality					
G1 aid	0.445			-1.038			0.361		
	(5.710)			(3.250)			(2.071)		
Non G1 aid	-1.209			0.0773			-1.181		
	(1.133)			(0.769)			(1.028)		
G2 aid		-0.295			-0.0689			-0.771	
		(2.735)			(1.276)			(2.507)	
Non G2 aid		-1.846			-0.0693			-0.744	
		(2.200)			(0.461)			(1.933)	
BA			0.589			0.0805			-0.528
			(1.378)			(1.200)			(0.419)
MA			-2.937			-0.176			-1.323
			(2.774)			(1.499)			(1.992)
Health expenditures	-0.0945	-0.0645	-0.0703	-0.0693	-0.0633	-0.0547	-0.0820*	-0.0720	-0.0721*
	(0.0592)	(0.0611)	(0.0646)	(0.0427)	(0.0482)	(0.0575)	(0.0453)	(0.0581)	(0.0423)
Urbanisation	0.127	-0.0900	0.0369	0.111	0.152	0.0959	0.000486	0.190	0.176
	(0.509)	(0.577)	(0.477)	(0.386)	(0.339)	(0.468)	(0.443)	(0.493)	(0.255)
Rural development	-4.72e-06	-5.68e-06**	-4.37e-06*	-7.22e-06**	-6.28e-06	-6.39e-06	-6.15e-06**	-5.02e-06	-4.78e-06*
	(2.90e-06)	(2.74e-06)	(2.47e-06)	(3.36e-06)	(3.86e-06)	(3.94e-06)	(2.82e-06)	(3.04e-06)	(2.51e-06)
Initial income	-0.577***	-0.514***	-0.622***	-0.453***	-0.509***	-0.498***	-0.489***	-0.560***	-0.559***
	(0.151)	(0.137)	(0.147)	(0.135)	(0.154)	(0.181)	(0.140)	(0.212)	(0.108)
Poverty	0.00722	0.00403	0.00423	0.00393	0.00223	0.00304	0.00673	0.00538	0.00582
	(0.00615)	(0.00487)	(0.00473)	(0.00436)	(0.00399)	(0.00528)	(0.00685)	(0.00602)	(0.00464)
Population growth	-0.0615	0.0498	-0.0557	0.0375	0.0605	0.0582	-0.0144	0.0423	0.0245
	(0.112)	(0.156)	(0.101)	(0.0804)	(0.0762)	(0.0664)	(0.129)	(0.0953)	(0.0976)
Institutional Quality	-0.103	-0.105*	-0.117	-0.109*	-0.143***	-0.127**	-0.112	-0.104	-0.101**
	(0.0878)	(0.0576)	(0.0881)	(0.0627)	(0.0498)	(0.0543)	(0.0745)	(0.0686)	(0.0432)
Political Instability	0.0130	-0.00836	0.00863	0.0313	0.00583	0.0183	0.00870	0.00855	0.00952
	(0.0462)	(0.0382)	(0.0289)	(0.0307)	(0.0303)	(0.0491)	(0.0442)	(0.0545)	(0.0390)
Constant	8.192***	8.327***	8.920***	7.060***	7.548***	7.515***	7.907***	7.543***	7.600***
	(2.445)	(2.291)	(1.930)	(1.471)	(1.334)	(1.477)	(1.503)	(1.575)	(0.968)
Observations	242	242	242	242	242	242	242	242	242
No. of recipient countries	82	82	82	82	82	82	82	82	82
No. of instruments	52	52	52	52	52	52	52	52	52
Hansen test p-value	0.194	0.361	0.576	0.538	0.713	0.588	0.741	0.479	0.637
AR(2)	0.346	0.222	0.431	0.217	0.199	0.124	0.456	0.622	0.491

Sources: Author's calculations.
Notes: The dependent variable is the average annual rate of infant mortality. Robust standard errors in parentheses. For descriptions of the variables and their sources, see appendix B1. ***, ** and * denote statistical significance at the 1%, 5%, and 10% level respectively.

Appendix F2: *The primary completion regressions*

	(1)	(2)	(3)	(4)	(5)	(6)	(7)	(8)	(9)
				Dependent variable: Primary completion					
G1 aid	-3.352			1.190			1.161		
	(4.832)			(2.687)			(2.829)		
Non G1 aid	-2.193*			-1.347			0.216		
	(1.273)			(1.293)			(1.013)		
G2 aid		-1.628			-2.148			-0.369	
		(2.752)			(3.038)			(2.029)	
Non G2 aid		-2.350			-1.914			0.404	
		(2.368)			(1.634)			(1.374)	
BA			-2.414			-2.661**			-1.707
			(1.936)			(1.176)			(1.656)
MA			-1.606			-0.0137			3.329
			(2.917)			(1.450)			(3.995)
Education expenditures	0.0190	0.0262	0.0153	0.0276	0.0238	0.0160	0.0168	0.0201	0.00562
	(0.0381)	(0.0377)	(0.0292)	(0.0292)	(0.0296)	(0.0251)	(0.0289)	(0.0274)	(0.0308)
Urbanisation	0.00541	-0.0319	-0.0836	0.265	-0.0930	0.0654	0.131	0.00803	0.0690
	(0.197)	(0.233)	(0.203)	(0.302)	(0.336)	(0.308)	(0.293)	(0.151)	(0.150)
Initial income	-0.0696	-0.0500	-0.0243	-0.00380	0.0537	0.0198	-0.00845	0.0207	0.0133
	(0.0934)	(0.103)	(0.110)	(0.102)	(0.0849)	(0.0829)	(0.0790)	(0.0931)	(0.0919)
Poverty	0.000215	-0.000794	0.000947	-0.00257	-0.000755	-0.000460	-0.00437	-0.00335	-0.00184
	(0.00447)	(0.00468)	(0.00566)	(0.00423)	(0.00542)	(0.00418)	(0.00332)	(0.00429)	(0.00476)
Population growth	-0.160**	-0.135*	-0.174**	-0.00556	-0.0379	-0.0636	-0.104	-0.124	-0.146
	(0.0797)	(0.0738)	(0.0826)	(0.0838)	(0.0797)	(0.0719)	(0.0805)	(0.0939)	(0.0905)
Institutional Quality	0.108	0.0987	0.0932	0.0966	0.161*	0.115	0.0742	0.0647	0.0649
	(0.109)	(0.112)	(0.0929)	(0.0813)	(0.0887)	(0.0722)	(0.0764)	(0.0665)	(0.0630)
Political Instability	0.00946	0.00392	0.0126	0.0122	0.0121	0.0199	0.0185	0.0195	0.0106
	(0.0182)	(0.0151)	(0.0191)	(0.0184)	(0.0203)	(0.0186)	(0.0155)	(0.0168)	(0.0175)
Constant	4.521***	4.523***	4.629***	2.808***	3.394**	3.390***	3.653***	3.972***	3.846***
	(1.019)	(1.204)	(1.181)	(0.931)	(1.310)	(1.073)	(0.997)	(0.916)	(0.867)
Observations	255	255	255	255	255	255	255	255	255
No. of recipient countries	82	82	82	82	82	82	82	82	82
No. of instruments	52	52	52	52	52	52	52	52	52
Hansen test p-value	0.143	0.166	0.207	0.222	0.0414	0.424	0.179	0.104	0.209
AR(2)	0.180	0.130	0.0789	0.0974	0.118	0.120	0.0541	0.0472	0.0661

Sources: Author's calculations.
Notes: The dependent variable is the average annual rate of primary completion. Robust standard errors in parentheses. For descriptions of the variables and their sources, see appendix B1. ***, ** and * denote statistical significance at the 1%, 5%, and 10% level respectively.

Appendix G: *Robustness tests - main regression*

Appendix G1: *Growth OLS and FE regressions - Whole period*

	Dependent variable: Average annual gdp growth per capita								
Estimator	(1) OLS	(2)	(3)	(4) FE	(5)	(6)	(7) FE	(8)	(9)
G1 aid	27.22***			21.03			32.21**		
	(8.721)			(16.91)			(12.80)		
Non G1 aid	-3.583			0.735			-3.422		
	(2.841)			(3.973)			(3.010)		
G2 aid		4.095			-10.05			-1.506	
		(24.19)			(8.444)			(6.932)	
Non G2 aid		18.98**			8.787**			1.253	
		(9.433)			(4.111)			(4.080)	
BA			0.728			-2.732			-0.968
			(11.31)			(5.813)			(5.110)
MA			42.76*			4.382			8.307
			(23.74)			(9.885)			(8.076)
Initial income	-0.845***	-0.749***	-0.731***	-4.465***	-4.465***	-4.489***	-4.641***	-4.509***	-4.421***
	(0.181)	(0.179)	(0.174)	(0.460)	(0.457)	(0.459)	(0.464)	(0.470)	(0.466)
Initial life expectancy	5.674***	5.565***	5.671***	-0.410	-0.368	-0.653	-0.724	-0.703	-1.032
	(1.451)	(1.442)	(1.457)	(2.051)	(2.044)	(2.061)	(2.052)	(2.074)	(2.069)
Geography	0.880***	0.871***	0.874***	0.993***	1.002***	0.962***	0.967***	0.962***	0.948***
	(0.158)	(0.159)	(0.159)	(0.168)	(0.168)	(0.169)	(0.167)	(0.168)	(0.168)
Institutional quality	0.0542*	0.0471*	0.0492*	0.0356*	0.0320	0.0244	0.0352*	0.0248	0.0249
	(0.0280)	(0.0284)	(0.0283)	(0.0214)	(0.0209)	(0.0211)	(0.0207)	(0.0204)	(0.0204)
Budget balance	0.0595	0.0610	0.0640	-0.144*	-0.135	-0.146*	-0.136	-0.147*	-0.158*
	(0.0676)	(0.0675)	(0.0677)	(0.0858)	(0.0858)	(0.0861)	(0.0857)	(0.0862)	(0.0864)
Political instability	0.304	0.226	0.230	2.314***	2.341***	2.450***	2.433***	2.435***	2.433***
	(0.245)	(0.247)	(0.244)	(0.505)	(0.504)	(0.504)	(0.495)	(0.498)	(0.497)
Trade to GDP	-0.00159**	-0.00161**	-0.00160**	-0.00122***	-0.00112**	-0.00107**	-0.000971**	-0.00110**	-0.00112**
	(0.000635)	(0.000630)	(0.000631)	(0.000445)	(0.000434)	(0.000440)	(0.000437)	(0.000437)	(0.000437)
Inflation	-0.000394	-0.000201	-0.000515	-3.83e-05	0.000221	0.000498	-0.000806	-0.000416	-0.000506
	(0.00164)	(0.00148)	(0.00134)	(0.00121)	(0.00133)	(0.00119)	(0.00164)	(0.00120)	(0.00146)
Constant	-18.38***	-18.47***	-19.06***	23.40***	23.03**	24.25***	25.87***	24.70***	25.36***
	(5.068)	(5.044)	(5.113)	(9.305)	(9.243)	(9.347)	(9.112)	(9.165)	(9.151)
Lag length	-	-	-	-		-		10 years	
Observations	570	570	570	570	570	570	570	570	570
No. of recipient countries	95	95	95	95	95	95	95	95	95
R-squared	0.283	0.274	0.275	0.372	0.374	0.368	0.377	0.368	0.370

Sources: Author's calculations.
Notes: The dependent variable is the average annual growth rate of GDP per capita. Robust standard errors in parentheses. For descriptions of the variables and their sources, see appendix B1. ***, ** and * denote statistical significance at the 1%, 5%, and 10% level respectively.

Appendix G2: *Growth OLS and FE regressions - Post-Cold War period*

	Dependent variable: Average annual gdp growth per capita								
Estimator	(1) OLS	(2)	(3)	(4) FE	(5)	(6)	(7) FE	(8)	(9)
G1 aid	61.17***			44.43**			31.14**		
	(22.58)			(22.28)			(15.12)		
Non G1 aid	-12.86***			-7.425			0.383		
	(4.402)			(5.497)			(3.966)		
G2 aid		-11.18			1.088			-4.288	
		(10.89)			(10.99)			(9.383)	
Non G2 aid		-0.649			0.645			8.666*	
		(5.332)			(5.729)			(5.011)	
BA			-2.617			-0.296			4.713
			(6.806)			(6.670)			(6.125)
MA			-4.199			3.446			5.470
			(8.896)			(12.10)			(9.790)
Initial income	-0.717***	-0.610***	-0.596***	-6.131***	-6.090***	-6.060***	-6.246***	-6.054***	-6.057***
	(0.216)	(0.218)	(0.223)	(0.813)	(0.821)	(0.830)	(0.815)	(0.812)	(0.814)
Initial life expectancy	3.235**	2.873*	3.050*	-1.370	-1.462	-1.463	-2.557	-2.367	-2.457
	(1.621)	(1.708)	(1.689)	(2.823)	(2.849)	(2.842)	(2.829)	(2.839)	(2.847)
Geography	0.796***	0.892***	0.884***	1.478***	1.509***	1.517***	1.543***	1.484***	1.455***
	(0.193)	(0.194)	(0.194)	(0.301)	(0.305)	(0.302)	(0.296)	(0.294)	(0.296)
Institutional quality	0.0491	0.0413	0.0443	0.0473*	0.0401	0.0399	0.0476*	0.0394	0.0381
	(0.0328)	(0.0335)	(0.0334)	(0.0264)	(0.0263)	(0.0264)	(0.0259)	(0.0254)	(0.0255)
Budget balance	0.0766	0.0866	0.0885	-0.178	-0.165	-0.161	-0.154	-0.169	-0.175
	(0.0850)	(0.0866)	(0.0874)	(0.143)	(0.144)	(0.145)	(0.143)	(0.143)	(0.143)
Political instability	0.0872	-0.0115	-0.0513	1.328*	1.329*	1.333*	1.370*	1.348*	1.330*
	(0.287)	(0.287)	(0.283)	(0.768)	(0.773)	(0.773)	(0.762)	(0.765)	(0.766)
Trade to GDP	-0.00260***	-0.00203*	-0.00210*	-0.00131**	-0.00104*	-0.00102	-0.000852	-0.000995	-0.00101*
	(0.000979)	(0.00114)	(0.00111)	(0.000620)	(0.000614)	(0.000618)	(0.000605)	(0.000605)	(0.000610)
Inflation	-0.000394	-0.000201	-0.000515	-3.83e-05	0.000221	0.000498	-0.000806	-0.000416	-0.000506
	(0.00164)	(0.00148)	(0.00134)	(0.00121)	(0.00133)	(0.00119)	(0.00164)	(0.00120)	(0.00146)
Constant	-10.84**	-10.54*	-11.30*	23.40***	23.03**	24.25***	25.87***	24.70***	25.36***
	(5.487)	(5.879)	(5.815)	(9.305)	(9.243)	(9.347)	(9.112)	(9.165)	(9.151)
Lag length	-	-	-	-				10 years	
Observations	392	392	392	570	570	570	570	570	570
No. of recipient countries	95	95	95	95	95	95	95	95	95
R-squared	0.251	0.226	0.225	0.354	0.345	0.345	0.357	0.353	0.350

Sources: Author's calculations.
Notes: The dependent variable is the average annual growth rate of GDP per capita with the observation period changed to 1990-2014. Robust standard errors in parentheses. For descriptions of the variables and their sources, see appendix B1. ***, ** and * denote statistical significance at the 1%, 5%, and 10% level respectively.

Appendix G3: *Infant mortality OLS and FE regressions*

	Dependent variable: Infant mortality					
	(1) OLS	(2)	(3)	(4) FE	(5)	(6)
G1 Aid	-0.629 (4.607)			**2.990** (3.195)		
Non G1 Aid	-0.603 (0.800)			0.549 (0.513)		
G2 Aid		-0.268 (2.077)			**2.111**** (0.998)	
Non G2 Aid		-0.743 (1.038)			0.255 (0.524)	
BA			-1.982 (1.553)			**1.147*** (0.668)
MA			1.043 (1.920)			**0.409** (0.741)
Health expenditures	-0.0667*** (0.0253)	-0.0666*** (0.0249)	-0.0679*** (0.0245)	-0.0110 (0.0133)	-0.00982 (0.0132)	-0.0101 (0.0133)
Urbanisation	0.200** (0.0913)	0.199** (0.0898)	0.212** (0.0900)	-0.234* (0.130)	-0.278** (0.130)	-0.251* (0.129)
Rural development	-9.76e-06*** (2.87e-06)	-9.77e-06*** (2.86e-06)	-9.78e-06*** (2.90e-06)	-1.98e-06** (9.35e-07)	-2.05e-06** (9.32e-07)	-1.99e-06** (9.36e-07)
Initial income	-0.301*** (0.0567)	-0.301*** (0.0563)	-0.300*** (0.0560)	-0.266*** (0.0630)	-0.275*** (0.0632)	-0.273*** (0.0641)
Poverty	0.00907*** (0.00240)	0.00901*** (0.00243)	0.00942*** (0.00246)	0.00127 (0.00118)	0.000798 (0.00123)	0.00109 (0.00120)
Population growth	0.189*** (0.0285)	0.189*** (0.0286)	0.188*** (0.0283)	-0.0543** (0.0253)	-0.0521** (0.0252)	-0.0530** (0.0252)
Institutional Quality	-0.0900*** (0.0307)	-0.0900*** (0.0303)	-0.0899*** (0.0304)	-0.0351 (0.0216)	-0.0376* (0.0214)	-0.0357* (0.0215)
Political Instability	0.0130 (0.0475)	0.000713 (0.0315)	-0.00524 (0.0609)	0.0117 (0.0318)	0.0145 (0.0413)	0.00370 (0.0414)
Constant	5.162*** (0.444)	5.164*** (0.443)	5.105*** (0.448)	6.436*** (0.651)	6.689*** (0.663)	6.554*** (0.654)
Observations	243	243	243	243	243	243
No. of recipient countries	83	83	83	83	83	83
R-squared	0.822	0.822	0.823	0.911	0.912	0.911
Variables dropped	-	-	-	-	-	-

(Continuation)

	Dependent variable: Infant mortality		
Estimator	(7) FE	(8)	(9)
G1	0.965 (1.674)		
Non G1	-0.877** (0.386)		
G2 Aid		-2.933*** (0.829)	
Non G2 Aid		0.570 (0.499)	
BA			-1.210** (0.546)
MA			0.0233 (0.812)
Education expenditures	0.0450*** (0.00969)	0.0442*** (0.00960)	0.0448*** (0.00969)
Urbanisation	0.354*** (0.0722)	0.326*** (0.0718)	0.330*** (0.0738)
Initial income	-0.120*** (0.0411)	-0.112*** (0.0407)	-0.118*** (0.0411)
Poverty			
Population growth	0.0394** (0.0198)	0.0376* (0.0195)	0.0420** (0.0198)
Institutional Quality			
Political Instability	0.00923 (0.0177)	0.00811 (0.0153)	0.0165 (0.0133)
Constant	3.788*** (0.394)	3.832*** (0.391)	3.852*** (0.396)
Observations	483	483	483
No. of recipient countries	93	93	93
R-squared	0.554	0.563	0.555
Variables dropped		poverty , institutional quality	

Sources: Author's calculations.
Notes: The dependent variable is the average annual rate of infant mortality. Robust standard errors in parentheses. For descriptions of the variables and their sources, see appendix B1. ***, ** and * denote statistical significance at the 1%, 5%, and 10% level respectively.

Appendix G4: *Primary Completion OLS and FE regressions*

Dependent variable: Primary completion

	(1) OLS	(2)	(3)	(4) FE	(5)	(6)	(7) FE	(8)	(9)
G1 aid	3.731*			0.353			0.965		
	(2.036)			(1.678)			(1.674)		
Non G1 aid	-2.031***			-1.705***			-0.877**		
	(0.533)			(0.565)			(0.386)		
G2 aid		-3.178**			-3.017***			-2.933***	
		(1.604)			(0.896)			(0.829)	
Non G2 aid		-0.0751			-0.0656			0.570	
		(0.804)			(0.657)			(0.499)	
BA			-1.065			-1.837***			-1.210**
			(0.772)			(0.504)			(0.546)
MA			-1.199			0.283			0.0233
			(1.069)			(0.978)			(0.812)
Education expenditures	0.0204**	0.0176**	0.0184**	0.0126	0.00944	0.00772	0.0450***	0.0442***	0.0448***
	(0.00802)	(0.00819)	(0.00797)	(0.0112)	(0.0110)	(0.0112)	(0.00969)	(0.00960)	(0.00969)
Urbanisation	0.0135	0.0206	0.00983	0.329**	0.369***	0.344**	0.354***	0.326***	0.330***
	(0.0385)	(0.0379)	(0.0381)	(0.137)	(0.136)	(0.136)	(0.0722)	(0.0718)	(0.0738)
Initial income	0.0624**	0.0731***	0.0765***	-0.153**	-0.117*	-0.135**	-0.120***	-0.112***	-0.118***
	(0.0271)	(0.0261)	(0.0252)	(0.0643)	(0.0663)	(0.0652)	(0.0411)	(0.0407)	(0.0411)
Poverty	-0.000432	-0.000429	-0.000517	0.00233	0.00285*	0.00260*			
	(0.00122)	(0.00124)	(0.00129)	(0.00144)	(0.00145)	(0.00145)			
Population growth	-0.0999***	-0.0993***	-0.0982***	-0.0311	-0.0373	-0.0347	0.0394**	0.0376*	0.0420**
	(0.0160)	(0.0163)	(0.0166)	(0.0311)	(0.0310)	(0.0310)	(0.0198)	(0.0195)	(0.0198)
Institutional Quality	0.0767***	0.0811***	0.0831***	0.0625***	0.0601***	0.0598***			
	(0.0184)	(0.0183)	(0.0190)	(0.0188)	(0.0187)	(0.0188)			
Political Instability	0.00221	0.00753		-0.00362	0.00246	-0.00969	0.00923	0.00811	0.0165
	(0.0190)	(0.0190)		(0.0278)	(0.0346)	(0.0314)	(0.0177)	(0.0153)	(0.0133)
Constant	3.355***	3.224***	3.206***	4.008***	3.585***	3.824***	3.788***	3.832***	3.852***
	(0.251)	(0.250)	(0.246)	(0.710)	(0.736)	(0.718)	(0.394)	(0.391)	(0.396)
Observations	256	256	256	256	256	256	483	483	483
No. of recipient countries	83	83	83	83	83	83	93	93	93
R-squared	0.663	0.658	0.652	0.583	0.592	0.585	0.554	0.563	0.555
Variables dropped	-	-	-	-	-	-	poverty , institutional quality		

Sources: Author's calculations.
Notes: The dependent variable is the average annual rate of primary completion. Robust standard errors in parentheses. For descriptions of the variables and their sources, see appendix B1. ***, ** and * denote statistical significance at the 1%, 5%, and 10% level respectively.

Appendix H: *Additional tests for robustness*

Appendix H1: *Difference GMM Robustness: Growth whole period*

Dependent variable: Average annual gdp growth per capita

Lag length	(1) 5 years	(2)	(3)	(4) 10 years	(5)	(6)	(7) 15 years	(8)	(9)
G1 aid	15.20			33.15**			15.96		
	(22.80)			(15.09)			(16.33)		
Non G1 aid	10.24			-1.989			1.300		
	(8.054)			(6.301)			(6.385)		
G2 aid		16.79			-4.200			-14.89	
		(15.50)			(13.23)			(15.37)	
Non G2 aid		8.138			5.995			8.640	
		(7.003)			(9.477)			(9.497)	
BA			7.553			4.263			-1.029
			(9.595)			(8.649)			(8.665)
MA			33.40*			-2.798			15.21
			(18.82)			(21.28)			(19.57)
Initial income	-5.232***	-4.186***	-5.221***	-5.606***	-4.583***	-4.765***	-5.184***	-4.753***	-4.802***
	(1.625)	(1.440)	(1.740)	(1.719)	(1.322)	(1.535)	(1.864)	(1.595)	(1.678)
Initial life expectancy	-4.068	-3.242	-5.767	-4.092	-3.791	-1.924	-3.396	-2.347	-2.822
	(6.208)	(5.296)	(5.992)	(5.233)	(4.602)	(5.469)	(5.353)	(5.235)	(6.261)
Institutional quality	0.357	0.379	0.310	0.436	0.368	0.352	0.112	0.400	0.136
	(0.573)	(0.514)	(0.532)	(0.526)	(0.522)	(0.537)	(0.587)	(0.540)	(0.569)
Budget balance	0.0434	0.0438	0.0783	0.0929	0.0514	0.0969	0.0375	0.0108	0.0419
	(0.0986)	(0.0694)	(0.0818)	(0.0768)	(0.0843)	(0.0834)	(0.0800)	(0.102)	(0.0883)
Political instability	-0.358*	-0.296	-0.422*	-0.360*	-0.307	-0.293	-0.391*	-0.300	-0.346
	(0.197)	(0.219)	(0.223)	(0.201)	(0.220)	(0.207)	(0.207)	(0.209)	(0.209)
Trade to GDP	3.328	3.159	3.663*	3.565**	2.929	4.216**	3.922**	3.814*	4.827**
	(2.143)	(2.015)	(1.951)	(1.687)	(1.992)	(2.026)	(1.866)	(1.981)	(2.049)
Inflation	-0.000666	-0.000618	-0.000929	6.38e-05	-0.000677	-0.000317	-0.000283	-0.000525	-0.000437
	(0.00110)	(0.00110)	(0.00111)	(0.00101)	(0.00109)	(0.00116)	(0.00123)	(0.00118)	(0.00136)
Observations	442	442	442	442	442	442	442	442	442
No. of recipient countries	78	78	78	78	78	78	78	78	78
No. of instruments	72	72	72	72	72	72	72	72	72
Hansen test p-value	0.582	0.437	0.680	0.344	0.339	0.257	0.332	0.204	0.502
AR(2)	0.752	0.764	0.511	0.922	0.959	0.911	0.871	0.888	0.747

Sources: Author's calculations.
Notes: The dependent variable is the average annual rate of GDP per capita growth. Robust standard errors in parentheses. For descriptions of the variables and their sources, see appendix B1. Eight time lags of the endogenous variables are considered. ***, ** and * denote statistical significance at the 1%, 5%, and 10% level respectively.

Appendix H2: *Difference GMM Robustness: Growth post-Cold War period*

Dependent variable: Average annual gdp growth per capita

Lag length	(1) 5 years	(2)	(3)	(4) 10 years	(5)	(6)	(7) 15 years	(8)	(9)
G1 aid	**8.612**			**37.61***			**21.56**		
	(23.13)			(14.13)			(17.64)		
Non G1 aid	10.89			-3.661			0.0225		
	(9.846)			(4.524)			(5.977)		
G2 aid		**25.51***			**-12.43**			**-22.67**	
		(14.72)			(15.61)			(17.47)	
Non G2 aid		4.781			9.473			10.02	
		(6.938)			(8.014)			(6.785)	
BA			**10.17**			**6.295**			**4.955**
			(8.109)			(7.566)			(9.498)
MA			**20.08**			**-1.279**			**3.093**
			(13.48)			(14.98)			(15.72)
Initial income	-5.160***	-4.796***	-5.586***	-6.113***	-5.112***	-5.805***	-6.010***	-5.589***	-6.099***
	(1.526)	(1.563)	(1.555)	(1.641)	(1.545)	(1.454)	(1.690)	(1.484)	(1.544)
Initial life expectancy	-2.888	-2.762	-4.614	-3.833	-3.137	-5.340	-6.121	-4.504	-6.659
	(4.889)	(4.643)	(4.444)	(4.120)	(3.845)	(3.949)	(4.435)	(3.665)	(4.055)
Institutional quality	0.410	0.465	0.468	0.509	0.415	0.428	0.350	0.634	0.255
	(0.426)	(0.434)	(0.402)	(0.421)	(0.440)	(0.422)	(0.516)	(0.473)	(0.471)
Budget balance	0.000888	0.0231	0.0351	0.0532	0.0437	0.0356	-0.0215	0.00156	-0.00346
	(0.0736)	(0.0560)	(0.0714)	(0.0596)	(0.0671)	(0.0604)	(0.0595)	(0.0673)	(0.0636)
Political instability	-0.332*	-0.319	-0.377*	-0.340*	-0.286	-0.355*	-0.405**	-0.282	-0.409**
	(0.188)	(0.201)	(0.196)	(0.172)	(0.189)	(0.189)	(0.192)	(0.199)	(0.194)
Trade to GDP	2.187	1.921	2.496	2.633**	2.462	3.194**	2.922*	2.873*	3.221**
	(1.480)	(1.585)	(1.602)	(1.315)	(1.484)	(1.440)	(1.470)	(1.557)	(1.523)
Inflation	-0.000211	-4.06e-05	-0.000162	0.000277	-0.000158	0.000123	-0.000109	-0.000209	-0.000226
	(0.000922)	(0.000826)	(0.000795)	(0.000867)	(0.00108)	(0.00104)	(0.00112)	(0.000989)	(0.00118)
Observations	330	330	330	330	330	330	330	330	330
No. of recipient countries	78	78	78	78	78	78	78	78	78
No. of instruments	68	68	68	68	68	68	68	68	68
Hansen test p-value	0.415	0.464	0.362	0.356	0.491	0.616	0.530	0.442	0.436
AR(2)	0.303	0.378	0.319	0.417	0.523	0.282	0.454	0.323	0.431

Sources: Author's calculations.
Notes: The dependent variable is the average annual rate of GDP per capita growth. Robust standard errors in parentheses. For descriptions of the variables and their sources, see appendix B1. Eight time lags of the endogenous variables are considered. ***, ** and * denote statistical significance at the 1%, 5%, and 10% level respectively.

Appendix H3: *GMM Robustness: The effect on infant mortality*

Dependent variable: Infant Mortality

	(1)	(2)	(3)	(4)	(5)	(6)	(7)	(8)	(9)
G1 aid	**-1.950**			**-16.58**			**-3.313**		
	(5.558)			(12.53)			(4.474)		
Non G1 aid	0.156			4.941**			-0.351		
	(1.164)			(2.449)			(1.437)		
G2 aid		**2.488**			**8.235***			**2.752**	
		(1.616)			(4.921)			(2.692)	
Non G2 aid		-0.999			-0.624			-1.967	
		(1.570)			(3.579)			(1.366)	
BA			**1.979**			**6.510**			**0.664**
			(3.151)			(4.874)			(1.108)
MA			**-5.730**			**-3.823**			**-4.073**
			(3.589)			(4.855)			(2.835)
Health expenditures	-0.0567	-0.0958**	-0.0428	-0.240**	-0.218**	-0.209**			
	(0.0369)	(0.0422)	(0.0621)	(0.112)	(0.103)	(0.0909)			
Urbanisation	0.305	0.296	0.0881	-0.0409	-0.00511	-0.212	0.344**	0.361*	0.286
	(0.279)	(0.254)	(0.381)	(0.374)	(0.344)	(0.360)	(0.170)	(0.191)	(0.200)
Rural development	-4.76e-06*	-4.08e-06*	-4.36e-06*	-9.16e-06*	-9.94e-06**	-1.09e-05**	-7.75e-06**	-8.55e-06**	-8.18e-06*
	(2.60e-06)	(2.31e-06)	(2.32e-06)	(4.66e-06)	(3.97e-06)	(4.17e-06)	(3.97e-06)	(3.93e-06)	(4.13e-06)
Initial income	-0.588***	-0.564***	-0.610***				-0.596***	-0.529***	-0.565***
	(0.115)	(0.133)	(0.147)				(0.108)	(0.116)	(0.133)
Poverty	0.00369	0.00549	0.00392	0.0143**	0.0154**	0.0112	0.000996	0.00373	0.00144
	(0.00359)	(0.00373)	(0.00618)	(0.00638)	(0.00695)	(0.00692)	(0.00389)	(0.00455)	(0.00549)
Population growth	0.0541	-9.98e-05	0.0378	0.0366	0.0599	0.0644	0.138	0.130	0.135
	(0.0689)	(0.114)	(0.0951)	(0.153)	(0.167)	(0.115)	(0.0907)	(0.0830)	(0.107)
Institutional Quality	-0.119**	-0.124***	-0.127**	-0.0919	-0.131	-0.182	-0.156**	-0.121**	-0.131*
	(0.0551)	(0.0452)	(0.0606)	(0.110)	(0.110)	(0.146)	(0.0781)	(0.0568)	(0.0757)
Political Instability	0.0130	0.000713	-0.00524	0.0117	0.0145	0.00370	0.00665	0.00806	0.00569
	(0.0475)	(0.0315)	(0.0609)	(0.0318)	(0.0413)	(0.0414)	(0.0370)	(0.0384)	(0.0280)
Constant	7.374***	7.440***	8.454***	4.319**	4.385***	5.597***	7.335***	6.495***	7.188***
	(1.202)	(1.068)	(1.601)	(1.643)	(1.651)	(1.778)	(1.117)	(1.141)	(1.558)
Observations	242	242	242	242	242	242	334	334	334
No. of recipient countries	82	82	82	82	82	82	83	83	83
No. of instruments	52	52	52	52	52	52	55	55	55
Hansen test p-value	0.620	0.538	0.258	0.308	0.286	0.131	0.321	0.311	0.288
AR(2)	0.263	0.383	0.468	0.615	0.191	0.278	0.586	0.438	0.794
Variables dropped	-	-	-	Initial income			Health expenditures		

Sources: Author's calculations.
Notes: The dependent variable is the average annual rate of infant mortality. Robust standard errors in parentheses. For descriptions of the variables and their sources, see appendix B1. ***, ** and * denote statistical significance at the 1%, 5%, and 10% level respectively.

Appendix H4: *GMM Robustness: The effect on primary completion*

	(1)	(2)	(3)	(4)	(5)	(6)	(7)	(8)	(9)
				Dependent variable: Primary completion					
G1 aid	**0.679**			**2.180**			**-0.124**		
	(5.719)			(4.631)			(4.371)		
Non G1 aid	-1.306			-3.110**			-1.654		
	(2.299)			(1.347)			(1.414)		
G2 aid		**-1.231**			**-8.117*****			**-3.466**	
		(3.946)			(3.086)			(2.840)	
Non G2 aid		-1.631			0.267			-0.653	
		(2.780)			(1.024)			(1.601)	
BA			**-4.009**			**-6.792****			**-2.564****
			(3.632)			(3.189)			(1.024)
MA			**2.236**			**-0.620**			**0.222**
			(3.452)			(3.556)			(1.704)
Education expenditures	0.0283	0.0119	0.0299	0.0391*	0.0399	0.0370	0.0209	-0.00534	-0.00288
	(0.0407)	(0.0344)	(0.0402)	(0.0205)	(0.0281)	(0.0360)	(0.0220)	(0.0215)	(0.0212)
Urbanisation	-0.0935	-0.103	-0.0225	0.336*	0.329	0.110	0.164	0.0626	0.121
	(0.171)	(0.227)	(0.257)	(0.182)	(0.221)	(0.171)	(0.187)	(0.214)	(0.228)
Initial income	0.00936	-0.0196	0.0242						
	(0.0901)	(0.0783)	(0.0964)						
Poverty	-0.00199	-0.00355	0.000156				-0.00255	-0.00257	-0.00151
	(0.00408)	(0.00383)	(0.00468)				(0.00264)	(0.00230)	(0.00222)
Population growth	-0.125*	-0.110	-0.139*	-0.0494	-0.0761	-0.0407	-0.0876	-0.120***	-0.130***
	(0.0745)	(0.0698)	(0.0698)	(0.0689)	(0.0552)	(0.0564)	(0.0535)	(0.0393)	(0.0399)
Institutional Quality	0.0485	0.0414	0.0785						
	(0.0776)	(0.0704)	(0.0761)						
Political Instability	0.00221	0.00753		-0.00362	0.00246	-0.00969	0.00923	0.00811	0.0165
	(0.0190)	(0.0190)		(0.0278)	(0.0346)	(0.0314)	(0.0177)	(0.0153)	(0.0133)
Constant	4.557***	4.957***	3.946***	3.176***	3.227***	4.056***	3.957***	4.506***	4.252***
	(0.873)	(0.935)	(1.274)	(0.761)	(0.935)	(0.759)	(0.746)	(0.871)	(0.956)
Observations	255	255	256	491	491	491	280	280	280
No. of recipient countries	82	82	83	93	93	93	84	84	84
No. of instruments	52	52	52	54	54	54	52	52	52
Hansen test p-value	0.400	0.341	0.333	0.106	0.0792	0.0919	0.386	0.534	0.569
AR(2)	0.118	0.113	0.0791	0.0518	0.101	0.110	0.514	0.353	0.483
Variables dropped	-	-	-	Initial income, poverty, institutional quality			initial income, institutional quality		

Sources: Author's calculations.
Notes: The dependent variable is the average annual rate of primary completion. Robust standard errors in parentheses. For descriptions of the variables and their sources, see appendix B1. ***, ** and * denote statistical significance at the 1%, 5%, and 10% level respectively.

Appendix I: *Hausman specification tests*

Appendix I1: *Hausman test (FE/RE) for the growth regression*

	(b)	(B)	(b-B)	sqrt(diag(V_b-V_B))
	fe	re	Difference	S.E.
initial_in e	-3.299552	-0.9909912	-2.308561	0.3062738
initial_le	-2.230585	1.231227	-3.461812	0.9232868
ec_freedom	0.9654969	0.7084507	0.2570462	0.0376675
polit_inst y	-0.290302	-0.1427859	-0.1475161	0.0266411
trade_gdp	2.623906	0.8164639	1.807442	0.3204555
inflation	-0.0010912	-0.0011704	0.0000792	.
ba_g1	4.607485	25.20458	-20.5971	6.984492
ba_n_g1	-1.897541	-7.580967	5.683425	1.8074

b = consistent under Ho and Ha; obtained from xtreg

B = inconsistent under Ha, efficient under Ho; obtained from xtreg

Test: Ho: difference in coefficients not systematic

chi2(7) = (b-B)'[(V_b-V_B)^(-1)](b-B)

= 114.25

Prob>chi2 = 0.0000

(V_b-V_B is not positive definite)

Appendix I2: *Hausman test (FE/RE) for the infant mortality regression*

	(b)	(B)	(b-B)	sqrt(diag(V_b-V_B))
	fe	re	Difference	S.E.
health_exp	-0.0605166	-0.10694	0.0464235	0.0020919
urbanisation	-0.7952816	-0.1064965	-0.6887851	0.1197229
rural_deve t	-0.00000468	-0.00000594	0.00000125	.
initial_in e	-0.6464951	-0.3672691	-0.279226	0.0428781
poverty_he t	0.0021175	0.006781	-0.0046635	.
ec_freedom	-0.0461759	-0.1028829	0.056707	.
polit_inst y	0.0082592	0.0072049	0.0010544	.
ba_g1	0.2755517	4.657112	-4.38156	.
ba_n_g1	1.436095	1.161619	0.2744764	.

b = consistent under Ho and Ha; obtained from xtreg

B = inconsistent under Ha, efficient under Ho; obtained from xtreg

Test: Ho: difference in coefficients not systematic

$chi2(8) = (b-B)'[(V\_b-V\_B)^{(-1)}](b-B)$

= 141.15

Prob>chi2 = 0.0000

(V_b-V_B is not positive definite)

Appendix I3: *Hausman test (FE/RE) for the primary completion regression*

	(b)	(B)	(b-B)	sqrt(diag(V_b-V_B))
	fe	re	Difference	S.E.
education_ p	0.0247159	0.0279251	-0.0032092	0.0070166
urbanisation	0.5235714	0.134291	0.3892804	0.1144524
initial_in e	0.0045265	0.0476671	-0.0431406	0.0475575
poverty_he t	0.0016961	-0.0009442	0.0026402	0.0009572
ec_freedom	0.0580056	0.0837492	-0.0257436	0.0094745
polit_inst y	0.0032134	0.0078935	-0.00468	0.0044216
ba_g1	1.873627	1.437461	0.4361659	0.7018081
ba_n_g1	-2.626951	-2.245625	-0.3813265	0.3039175

b = consistent under Ho and Ha; obtained from xtreg

B = inconsistent under Ha, efficient under Ho; obtained from xtreg

Test: Ho: difference in coefficients not systematic

$chi2(8) = (b-B)'[(V\_b-V\_B)^{(-1)}](b-B)$

= 25.29

Prob>chi2 = 0.0014

(V_b-V_B is not positive definite)

References

Alesina, A. and Dollar, D. (2000): 'Who Gives Foreign Aid to Whom and Why?', *Journal of Economic Growth* 5(1), 33–63.
   URL: *http://dx.doi.org/10.1023/A:1009874203400*

Alvi, E., Mukherjee, D. and Shukralla, E. K. (2008): 'Aid, Policies, and Growth in Developing Countries: A New Look at the Empirics', *Southern Economic Journal* 74(3), 693–706.
   URL: *http://www.jstor.org/stable/20111991*

Alvi, E. and Senbeta, A. (2012): 'Does foreign aid reduce poverty?', *Journal of International Development* 24(8), 955–976.
   URL: *http://dx.doi.org/10.1002/jid.1790*

Arndt, C., Jones, S. and Tarp, F. (2010): 'Aid, Growth, and Development: Have We Come Full Circle?', *Journal of Globalization and Development* 1(2), 1948–1837.
   URL: *https://doi.org/10.2202/1948-1837.1121*

Arndt, C., Jones, S. and Tarp, F. (2015): 'Assessing Foreign Aid's Long-Run Contribution to Growth and Development', *World Development* 69, 6 – 18. Aid Policy and the Macroeconomic Management of Aid.
   URL: *http://www.sciencedirect.com/science/article/pii/S0305750X13003008*

Bearce, D. H. and Tirone, D. C. (2010): 'Foreign Aid Effectiveness and the Strategic Goals of Donor Governments', *The Journal of Politics* 72(3), 837–851.
   URL: *http://dx.doi.org/10.1017/S0022381610000204*

Berthélemy, J.-C. (2006A): 'Bilateral Donors' Interest vs. Recipients' Development Motives in Aid Allocation: Do All Donors Behave the Same?', *Review of Development Economics* 10(2), 179–194.
   URL: *http://dx.doi.org/10.1111/j.1467-9361.2006.00311.x*

Berthélemy, J.-C. (2006B): 'Aid allocation: Comparing donors' behaviours', *Swedish Economic Policy Review* 13, 75–109.
   URL: *http://dx.doi.org/10.1111/j.1467-9361.2006.00311.x*

Bloom, D. E., Canning, D. and Sevilla, J. (2004): 'The Effect of Health on Economic Growth: A Production Function Approach', *World Development* 32(1), 1 – 13.
   URL: *http://www.sciencedirect.com/science/article/pii/S0305750X03001943*

Blundell, R. and Bond, S. (1998): 'Initial conditions and moment restrictions in dynamic panel data models', *Journal of Econometrics* 87(1), 115 – 143.
   URL: *http://www.sciencedirect.com/science/article/pii/S0304407698000098*

Boone, P. (1996): 'Politics and the effectiveness of foreign aid', *European Economic Review* 40(2), 289 – 329.
URL: *//www.sciencedirect.com/science/article/pii/0014292195001271*

Brückner, M. (2013): 'On the simultaneity problem in the aid and growth debate', *Journal of Applied Econometrics* 28(1), 126–150.
URL: *http://dx.doi.org/10.1002/jae.1259*

Burnside, C. and Dollar, D. (2000): 'Aid, Policies, and Growth', *American Economic Review* 90(4), 847–868.
URL: *http://www.aeaweb.org/articles?id=10.1257/aer.90.4.847*

Chong, A., Gradstein, M. and Calderon, C. (2009): 'Can foreign aid reduce income inequality and poverty?', *Public Choice* 140(1), 59–84.
URL: *http://dx.doi.org/10.1007/s11127-009-9412-4*

Clemens, M. A., Radelet, S. and Bhavnani, R. R. (2004): 'Counting Chickens When They Hatch: The Short Term Effect of Aid on Growth', *Center for Global Development working paper no. 44* .
URL: *https://ssrn.com/abstract=1112709*

Clemens, M. A., Radelet, S., Bhavnani, R. R. and Bazzi, S. (2012): 'Counting Chickens when they Hatch: Timing and the Effects of Aid on Growth*', *The Economic Journal* 122(561), 590–617.
URL: *http://dx.doi.org/10.1111/j.1468-0297.2011.02482.x*

Collier, P. and Dollar, D. (2001): 'Can the World Cut Poverty in Half? How Policy Reform and Effective Aid Can Meet International Development Goals', *World Development* 29(11), 1787 – 1802.
URL: *http://www.sciencedirect.com/science/article/pii/S0305750X01000766*

Collier, P. and Dollar, D. (2002): 'Aid allocation and poverty reduction', *European Economic Review* 46(8), 1475 – 1500.
URL: *//www.sciencedirect.com/science/article/pii/S0014292101001878*

Dalgaard, C.-J., Hansen, H. and Tarp, F. (2004): 'On The Empirics of Foreign Aid and Growth*', *The Economic Journal* 114(496), F191–F216.
URL: *http://dx.doi.org/10.1111/j.1468-0297.2004.00219.x*

DESA (Department of Economics and Social Affairs, UN) (2016): 'Sustainable Development Goals Report 2016', *United Nations* .
URL: *https://unstats.un.org/sdgs/report/2016/*

Djankov, S., Montalvo, J. G. and Reynal-Querol, M. (2008): 'The curse of aid', *Journal of Economic Growth* 13(3), 169–194.
URL: *http://dx.doi.org/10.1007/s10887-008-9032-8*

Dollar, D. and Levin, V. (2006): 'The Increasing Selectivity of Foreign Aid, 1984–2003', *World Development* 34(12), 2034 – 2046.
URL: *http://www.sciencedirect.com/science/article/pii/S0305750X06001549*

Doucouliagos, H. and Paldam, M. (2006): 'Aid Effectiveness on Accumulation: A Meta Study', *Kyklos* 59(2), 227–254.
URL: *http://dx.doi.org/10.1111/j.1467-6435.2006.00326.x*

Doucouliagos, H. and Paldam, M. (2009): 'THE AID EFFECTIVENESS LITERATURE: THE SAD RESULTS OF 40 YEARS OF RESEARCH', *Journal of Economic Surveys* 23(3), 433–461.
URL: *http://dx.doi.org/10.1111/j.1467-6419.2008.00568.x*

Dreher, A., Mölders, F. and Nunnenkamp, P. (2010): 'Aid Delivery through Non-governmental Organisations: Does the Aid Channel Matter for the Targeting of Swedish Aid?', *World Economy* 33(2), 147–176.
URL: *http://dx.doi.org/10.1111/j.1467-9701.2009.01233.x*

Dreher, A., Nunnenkamp, P. and Thiele, R. (2008): 'Does Aid for Education Educate Children? Evidence from Panel Data', *The World Bank Economic Review* 22(2), 291.
URL: + *http://dx.doi.org/10.1093/wber/lhn003*

Dreher, A., Nunnenkamp, P. and Thiele, R. (2011): 'Are 'New' Donors Different? Comparing the Allocation of Bilateral Aid Between nonDAC and {DAC} Donor Countries', *World Development* 39(11), 1950 – 1968. Expanding Our Understanding of Aid with a New Generation in Development Finance Information.
URL: *http://www.sciencedirect.com/science/article/pii/S0305750X11001999*

Easterly, W. (2003): 'Can Foreign Aid Buy Growth?', *The Journal of Economic Perspectives* 17(3), 23–48.
URL: *http://www.ingentaconnect.com/content/aea/jep/2003/00000017/00000003/art00002*

Easterly, W., Levine, R. and Roodman, D. (2004): 'Aid, Policies, and Growth: Comment', *American Economic Review* 94(3), 774–780.
URL: *http://www.aeaweb.org/articles?id=10.1257/0002828041464560*

Gates, S. and Hoeffler, A. (2004): 'Global Aid Allocation: Are Nordic Donors Different?', *No. 2004-34. Centre for the Study of African Economies, University of Oxford* .
URL: *https://ideas.repec.org/p/csa/wpaper/2004-34.html*

Gomanee, K., Girma, S. and Morrissey, O. (2005A): 'Aid and growth in Sub-Saharan Africa: accounting for transmission mechanisms', *Journal of International Development* 17(8), 1055–1075.
URL: *http://dx.doi.org/10.1002/jid.1259*

Gomanee, K., Girma, S. and Morrissey, O. (2005B): 'Aid, public spending and human welfare: evidence from quantile regressions', *Journal of International Development* 17(3), 299–309.
   URL: *http://dx.doi.org/10.1002/jid.1163*

Griffin, K. B. and Enos, J. L. (1970): 'Foreign Assistance: Objectives and Consequences', *Economic Development and Cultural Change* 18(3), 313–327.
   URL: *http://dx.doi.org/10.1086/450435*

Gwartney, J., Lawson, R., and Hall, J. (2016): 'Economic Freedom of the World 2016 Annual Report', *Fraser Institute* .
   URL: *https://www.fraserinstitute.org/studies/economic-freedom-of-the-world-2016-annual-report*

Hansen, H. and Tarp, F. (2001): 'Aid and growth regressions', *Journal of Development Economics* 64(2), 547 – 570.
   URL: *//www.sciencedirect.com/science/article/pii/S0304387800001504*

Harrigan, J. and Wang, C. (2011): 'A New Approach to the Allocation of Aid Among Developing Countries: Is the {USA} Different from the Rest?', *World Development* 39(8), 1281 – 1293.
   URL: *http://www.sciencedirect.com/science/article/pii/S0305750X11000052*

Hausman, J. A. (1978): 'Specification Tests in Econometrics', *Econometrica* 46(6), 1251–1271.
   URL: *http://www.jstor.org/stable/1913827*

Headey, D. (2008): 'Geopolitics and the effect of foreign aid on economic growth: 1970–2001', *Journal of International Development* 20(2), 161–180.
   URL: *http://dx.doi.org/10.1002/jid.1395*

Kilby, C. and Dreher, A. (2010): 'The impact of aid on growth revisited: Do donor motives matter?', *Economics Letters* 107(3), 338 – 340.
   URL: *http://www.sciencedirect.com/science/article/pii/S0165176510000789*

Kimura, H., Mori, Y. and Sawada, Y. (2012): 'Aid Proliferation and Economic Growth: A Cross-Country Analysis', *World Development* 40(1), 1 – 10.
   URL: *http://www.sciencedirect.com/science/article/pii/S0305750X11001409*

Kosack, S. (2003): 'Effective Aid: How Democracy Allows Development Aid to Improve the Quality of Life', *World Development* 31(1), 1 – 22.
   URL: *http://www.sciencedirect.com/science/article/pii/S0305750X02001778*

Levy, V. (1988): 'Aid and growth in Sub-Saharan Africa: The recent experience', *European Economic Review* 32(9), 1777 – 1795.
   URL: *http://www.sciencedirect.com/science/article/pii/0014292188900852*

Marshall, M. G. (2016): 'Major episodes of political violence (MEPV) and conflict regions, 1946-2015', *Center for Systemic Peace* .
URL: *http://www.systemicpeace.org/*

Masud, N. and Yontcheva, B. (2005): 'Does Foreign Aid Reduce Poverty? Empirical Evidence from Nongovernmental and Bilateral Aid', *International Monetary Fund Working Paper No. 05/100* .
URL: *http://www.imf.org/EXTERNAL/PUBS/CAT/longres.aspx?sk=17973.0*

McGillivray, M. (1991): 'The human development index: Yet another redundant composite development indicator?', *World Development* 19(10), 1461 – 1468.
URL: *http://www.sciencedirect.com/science/article/pii/0305750X9190088Y*

McKinlay, R. D. and Little, R. (1977): 'A Foreign Policy Model of U.S. Bilateral Aid Allocation', *World Politics* 30(1), 58–86.
URL: *https://doi.org/10.2307/2010075*

Minoiu, C. and Reddy, S. G. (2010): 'Development aid and economic growth: A positive long-run relation', *The Quarterly Review of Economics and Finance* 50(1), 27 – 39. Special Section: Foreign Aid.
URL: *http://www.sciencedirect.com/science/article/pii/S1062976909000969*

Mishra, P. and Newhouse, D. (2009): 'Does health aid matter?', *Journal of Health Economics* 28(4), 855 – 872.
URL: *http://www.sciencedirect.com/science/article/pii/S0167629609000563*

Mosley, P. (1980): 'Aid, savings and growth revisited', *Oxford Bulletin of Economics and Statistics* 42(2), 79–95.
URL: *http://dx.doi.org/10.1111/j.1468-0084.1980.mp42002002.x*

Mosley, P., Hudson, J. and Horrell, S. (1987): 'Aid, the Public Sector and the Market in Less Developed Countries', *The Economic Journal* 97(387), 616–641.
URL: *http://www.jstor.org/stable/2232927*

OECD, DAC (Development Assistance Comittee) (2016), 'Database on aid disbursements'.
URL: *http://stats.oecd.org/Index.aspx?datasetcode=TABLE2A*

Papanek, G. F. (1972): 'The Effect of Aid and Other Resource Transfers on Savings and Growth in Less Developed Countries', *The Economic Journal* 82(327), 934–950.
URL: *http://www.jstor.org/stable/2230259*

Papanek, G. F. (1973): 'Aid, Foreign Private Investment, Savings, and Growth in Less Developed Countries', *Journal of Political Economy* 81(1), 120–130.
URL: *http://dx.doi.org/10.1086/260009*

Pedersen, D. (2002): 'Political violence, ethnic conflict, and contemporary wars: broad implications for health and social well-being', *Social Science & Medicine* 55(2), 175 – 190.
URL: *http://www.sciencedirect.com/science/article/pii/S0277953601002611*

Rajan, R. G. and Subramanian, A. (2008): 'Aid and Growth: What Does the Cross-Country Evidence Really Show?', *Review of Economics and Statistics* 90(4), 643– 665.
URL: *http://dx.doi.org/10.1162/rest.90.4.643*

Roodman, D. (2007): 'The Anarchy of Numbers: Aid, Development, and Cross-Country Empirics', *The World Bank Economic Review* 21(2), 255–277.
URL: *http://dx.doi.org/10.1093/wber/lhm004*

Roodman, D. (2009A): 'How to do xtabond2: An introduction to difference and system GMM in Stata', *The Stata Journal* 9(1), 86–136.
URL: *http://dx.doi.org/10.1093/wber/lhm004*

Roodman, D. (2009B): 'A Note on the Theme of Too Many Instruments', *Oxford Bulletin of Economics and Statistics* 71(1), 135–158.
URL: *http://dx.doi.org/10.1111/j.1468-0084.2008.00542.x*

Rosenstein-Rodan, P. N. (1961): 'International Aid for Underdeveloped Countries', *The Review of Economics and Statistics* 43(2), 107–138.
URL: *http://www.jstor.org/stable/1928662*

Sachs, J. D., Warner, A., Åslund, A. and Fischer, S. (1995): 'Economic Reform and the Process of Global Integration', *Brookings Papers on Economic Activity* 1995(1), 1– 118.
URL: *http://www.jstor.org/stable/2534573*

Schraeder, P. J., Hook, S. W. and Taylor, B. (1998): 'Clarifying the Foreign Aid Puzzle: A Comparison of American, Japanese, French, and Swedish Aid Flows', *World Politics* 50(2), 294–323.
URL: *https://doi.org/10.1017/S0043887100008121*

Snyder, D. W. (1993): 'Donor bias towards small countries: an overlooked factor in the analysis of foreign aid and economic growth', *Applied Economics* 25(4), 481–488.
URL: *http://dx.doi.org/10.1080/00036849300000056*

Temple, J. R. (2010), Chapter 67 - Aid and Conditionality*, *in* D. Rodrik and M. Rosenzweig, eds, 'Handbooks in Economics', Vol. 5 of *Handbook of Development Economics*, Elsevier, pp. 4415 – 4523.
URL: *http://www.sciencedirect.com/science/article/pii/B9780444529442000057*

Tierney, M. J., Nielson, D. L., Hawkins, D. G., Roberts, J. T., Findley, M. G., Powers, R. M., Parks, B., Wilson, S. E. and Hicks, R. L. (2011): 'More Dollars than Sense: Refining Our Knowledge of Development Finance Using AidData', *World Development* 39(11), 1891 – 1906. Expanding Our Understanding of Aid with a New Generation in Development Finance Information.
URL: *http://www.sciencedirect.com/science/article/pii/S0305750X1100204X*

Trumbull, W. N. and Wall, H. J. (1994): 'Estimating Aid-Allocation Criteria with Panel Data', *The Economic Journal* 104(425), 876–882.
URL: *http://www.jstor.org/stable/2234981*

UNDP (United Nations Development Programme) (2003): 'The Millennium Development Goals', *in Human Development Report 2003: Millennium Development Goals – A Compact among Nations to End Human Poverty, UNDP* .
URL: *http://www.undp.org/content/undp/en/home/library.html*

Wacziarg, R. and Welch, K. H. (2008): 'Trade Liberalization and Growth: New Evidence', *The World Bank Economic Review* 22(2), 187.
URL: *http://dx.doi.org/10.1093/wber/lhn007*

Weisskopf, T. E. (1972): 'The impact of foreign capital inflow on domestic savings in underdeveloped countries', *Journal of International Economics* 2(1), 25 – 38.
URL: *//www.sciencedirect.com/science/article/pii/0022199672900438*

World Bank (2016), 'World Development Indicators'.
URL: *http://data.worldbank.org/data-catalog/world-development-indicators*